"Technology should not be held as the only way for society to advance. Here, *Urban Green* looks at other options. Neil Chambers provides a plan for action that goes beyond simply reducing our human activities and built environment's impact on nature. It indicates how nature could thrive in synchrony with society. It relooks at green building and speculates how civilization might extend into the future as the next generation of sustainability."

—Ken Yeang, architect, eco-architect, and author of
The Green Skyscraper, Ecodesign, and *EcoMasterplanning*

"Buildings, even 'green' buildings, have impacts that ripple across the infrastructures of towns, suburbs, and cities. Those ripples also have far-reaching and under-appreciated impacts on water, biodiversity, ecosystem services, and wilderness. Like a central stone at the summit of an arch or a predator maintaining biodiversity through strong species interactions, *Urban Green* is keystone: it melds the art (and science) of building design with the science of biodiversity conservation. A must-read for anyone chasing the architecture of the future."

—C. Josh Donlan, executive director, Advanced
Conservation Strategies and visiting fellow, Cornell University

"Neil Chambers' *Urban Green* is wide-ranging, imaginative, and at times ornery and irreverent. This is just what we need to help rethink building in our immediate future. Chambers makes clear that orthodoxy about 'green building' needs to be contextualized to take into account our development and use of energy, water, and space. More reflection and less impulsive action can go a long way in meeting many goals of an effective green movement."

—Martin V. Melosi, author of *The Sanitary City*

"If Hollywood ever got hold of Neil Chambers, the shear strength of his vision for the future would win an Oscar. Imaginary worlds by James Cameron pale in comparison to the realities Neil conceives by integrating the amazing complexity of ecology, energy, and technology into our built world. The most amazing thing is that Neil is not only dreaming, but making his vision real."

—Michael Guthrie, AIA, LEED AP, principal, inFORM studio

"Al Gore ain't got anything on Neil Chambers. Thousands of people talk about 'green' energy, but only a handful of people do anything about it. Neil is one of them. Personable and approachable, he is a genius with issues surrounding sustainable and green energy, and one of the authorities on the subject. Neil brings the subject to an accessible and exciting level, while maintaining a high knowledge value that incites change in us all."

—Brent Arnold, founder and creative director, More Than Us

"If you want to build a truly green world, Neil Chambers is a one-stop shop for all essential parts…always the smartest green guy in the room. When you listen to Neil explain how the future will be about sustainability—you know it can happen!"

—David Pollak, former cochair, New York State Democratic Party

"We live in a complex world that requires interdisciplinary solutions to address the challenges that lie ahead. Neil Chambers has the power, charisma, and intellectual capacity to not only envision a more equitable and sustainable world, but also the ability to bring together the diverse voices of those who will make that world a reality."

—Errol Mazursky, executive director,
Environmental Leadership Program

"In my twenty-two years of working with hundreds of green businesses and teaching environmental business at Columbia University and other institutions, Neil Chambers is in a league of his own. He not only understands the topics of sustainable cities and green buildings, but he can explain and articulate these complex and rapidly changing issues in a way that is easy to grasp and interesting to learn."

—Stefan Doering, president and founder, BEST Coaches, Inc.

"Having worked on some of the leading sustainable design projects in the world, I believe that Neil Chambers is one of the most dynamic environmental leaders I've met. I've always been impressed by the quality and range of work that Neil manages to engage in meaningfully on a professional level—design, media, political advocacy, and education."

—Chris Garvin, AIA, LEED-AP, partner, Terrapin Bright Green

"Quick on his feet, Neil Chambers has the uncanny ability to fuse some of the most challenging concepts in renewable energy into building integrated systems. Almost by instinct, he can rapidly visualize how any technology can effectively be adapted to the built environment. Whether it is a hydrogen generation system or wind or a solar technology, he can shape it into the fabric of the materials we use to form our communities."

—Mark Townsend Cox, founder and CEO, New Energy Fund LP

"There are very few people in the world who have the integrity and conviction backed up with absolute knowledge to align real-world work with core beliefs. Neil Chambers is one of those very few. Equally important is the generosity of spirit that he brings to the table. It is always about business, but it must first be about the greater good. That is Neil Chambers."

—Anthony Lilore, cofounder and design director, RESTORE CLOTHING

URBAN GREEN
ARCHITECTURE FOR THE FUTURE
NEIL B. CHAMBERS

palgrave
macmillan

URBAN GREEN

Copyright © Neil B. Chambers, 2011.

First published in 2011 by
PALGRAVE MACMILLAN®
in the United States—a division of St. Martin's Press LLC,
175 Fifth Avenue, New York, NY 10010.

Where this book is distributed in the UK, Europe and the rest of the world,
this is by Palgrave Macmillan, a division of Macmillan Publishers Limited,
registered in England, company number 785998, of Houndmills,
Basingstoke, Hampshire RG21 6XS.

Palgrave Macmillan is the global academic imprint of the above companies
and has companies and representatives throughout the world.

Palgrave® and Macmillan® are registered trademarks in the United States,
the United Kingdom, Europe and other countries.

ISBN: 978–0–230–10763–2

Library of Congress Cataloging-in-Publication Data

Chambers, Neil B.
    Urban Green : Architecture for the Future / Neil B. Chambers.
      pages cm
    Includes index.
    ISBN 978–0–230–10763–2
      1. Architecture—Environmental aspects. 2. Environmental protection.
    I. Title.
NA2542.35.C47 2011
720′.47—dc22   2010049320

A catalogue record of the book is available from the British Library.

Design by Newgen Imaging Systems (P) Ltd., Chennai, India.

First edition: July 2011

10 9 8 7 6 5 4 3 2 1

Printed in the United States of America.

To Lucy, my wife

Your continuous love shows me a better future for the planet is possible

CONTENTS

LIST OF FIGURES

URBAN GREEN

INTRODUCTION

WHY THE CURRENT GREEN MOVEMENT IS GETTING IT WRONG

When the A2B, a light electric bicycle manufactured by Ultra Motor, first came out in 2009, I reviewed it for treehugger.com. As I buzzed up and down the cobblestoned, lightly crowded blocks of lower Manhattan, I felt euphoric. This was no ordinary bicycle. With a slight turn of the hand grip, the electrical-powered engine pulled me forward in such a smooth way that it was more like swimming than riding a bike. Until that moment, I had never considered electric vehicles as a real alternative to other sources like petroleum. I went starry eyed thinking about how every person in New York City could replace taxi rides with e-bikes…my head quickly began to grasp the idea of the technology scaling up across all of the United States, then Canada, China, and Europe until finally the entire world was driving in or riding on electric vehicles! How glorious it would be if we all used electricity, I thought. Never again would we need the dirty fuels of the past for transportation like oil or the problems that come with it. After I was finished, I raced home, flipped on my laptop, and began my review. At the end of it, I stated: "If you wanna be a trendsetter and eco-friendly, this bike is for you. Plus, it's a super fun ride with easy mobility and high performance—what else could you ask for?"

I quickly uploaded the post to treehugger, added the essential elements like links and photos, and saved it to go live to the site. I felt great.

I got it. I had experienced firsthand the incredible future unfolding called the green revolution. A few hours later, I was still coming down from the euphoria. As I did, I could not help wondering if all my excitement was clouding my perspective. Would the world of tomorrow be safe in the hands of electric vehicles or for that matter green buildings (my area of expertise)? Could electric cars or energy-efficient buildings really create a sustainable society? For one, the electricity we use is not a naturally occurring product. It has to come from some other form, and most of the electricity in the United States comes from fossil fuels.

At first, I tried to disregard the notion of doubt as if it were a non-sensical idea or an immature impulse, but it would not go away. For more than 15 years at that time, I had committed myself to green design. Every day I had advocated and done everything I could to move the movement forward, and now after having one of the most fun experi-ences I'd ever had while riding what I hoped might potentially become the future of transportation, I was questioning it all. I sat in my apartment in the Lower East Side of New York puzzled by this haunting thought— is the green revolution really moving us toward a society of sustain-ability? Could simple changes in our decisions, such as to use electric transport instead of internal combustion engines, change everything? I was not sure, and not being sure gave me a moment of self-crisis. It would have been bad enough if I was only questioning alternative vehi-cles, but the idea had spread into everything I had held true for years. So I did what any self-respecting designer-journalist would do. I pulled out a piece of paper and tried to figure it out. I started by asking myself some basic questions, and then followed that up with about a thousand hours of research on topics like infrastructure, energy efficiency, renew-able energy, habitat restoration, old growth forests, and several other related subjects. These had always been within my professional area, and I had written about them in the past. But I had never questioned them or looked at them from the perspective of the bigger picture. What I found was astonishing and became the foundation for what you will read in the pages of this book.

The first thing I asked myself was what is green building? I have been asked that question thousands of times by students, designers, elected officials, architects, journalists, and just about everyone I work with. Most people have heard the term *green building*, but few could tell you what it is. Terms like *clean energy*, *renewable energy*, *sustainability*, and *geothermal* are just four that get thrown around without being well defined. Every time I am asked what green building is, and I try to give a short answer, such as "Green building is about saving energy and water and using sustainable materials," it proves incomplete to the person asking, because it only makes more questions come to mind such as "How do you save energy in a building?" "What do you mean by saving water?" or "What is a sustainable material?"

No short answer exists to define green building, nor does green building relate to merely one definition. To understand green building, it is best to look at it from three perspectives: First, we should understand what the current practices of green focus on. Second, we should consider if the practices of today's green buildings actually do what they say they are doing—namely, saving energy and water, and preserving and ultimately restoring nature. In looking at where green building stands today, we should also imagine where it needs to be in the next few decades to accomplish its goal of reducing the impact of humans on nature. Third, we should imagine the best-case scenario and envision a human world that has actually accomplished the aim of living in harmony with the natural world.

I think it could take at least 100 years to get to where we should be, so this third way of looking at green building is projected out into the next century. What I am hinting at is that green buildings alone cannot do everything. Buildings in general are greatly dependent on processes and systems that allow them to function. For example, you can't turn on your lights or television or faucet without infrastructure to support that action. In the bigger picture, green buildings are part of infrastructure, and by infrastructure I mean the energy grid, waterworks, and transportation systems. Current green building practices do not acknowledge buildings' dependencies on these larger systems, or how buildings' infrastructure impact the environment, or how poor infrastructure allows buildings to waste energy and water. So, to solve the problems caused by buildings, we can't focus just on individual buildings. We must do much more to live in harmony with nature.

Those are the three ways I discuss green building in this book. The odd thing is that I have never been asked another, much more basic question: "What is a building?" Green builders and designers assume everyone knows what green means and why green buildings are important, but I would argue that most people do not. In fact, most people do not know what a building actually is. You may think a building is a house or an office or a mall. But this is a very limited view that takes into account only the end result of a much larger process. In the first section of the book, I explain what a building really is as well as give a clear understanding of the most common current practices in the field of green building. In general, green architecture focuses only on the building at hand. The attention on individual buildings means other topics like cities, roadways, and other infrastructure are ignored, but these things have greater unintentional negative impacts on the environment than do single structures.

The negative impact caused by infrastructure is a serious problem facing the natural world and all things living in it, such as deer, raccoons, frogs, and tigers, as well as us. Habitat is disappearing, species are at the brink of extinction, and wilderness is becoming something of the past: literally, nature is being erased from the face of the planet with the construction of one building at a time. As more and more natural areas are replaced with artificial areas (for example, wetlands with parking lots), the ecological services that nature provides to us for free are eliminated. For example, trees filter the air to make it cleaner, but we have lost nearly 30 percent of all forests to houses, office parks, and other buildings in America. Worldwide, more than half of all the natural lands have been destroyed. Watersheds channel water in ways that cleanse it and improve its quality. Mangroves protect coastal areas against storm surges from hurricanes, and wetlands prevent floods. However, real estate development in America has replaced more than 50 percent of all wetlands with buildings. Green building today does not address the need to preserve wetlands or watersheds or other ecological services. But that is only part of the story. The pollution caused from making all the materials that go into a buildings has a bigger effect on the environment than do all the materials that end up in the building itself. The first few chapters look at expanding the view of what a building is to include the impact of infrastructure on the natural world.

Within the middle chapters of the book, I explore how the current practices of green building could be expanded to include cities and infrastructure to become green buildings of tomorrow. The transformation of buildings, highways, and urban areas into green structures cannot alone be the responsibility of designers, architects, and engineers. An entire area of science is dedicated to conserving and restoring nature, namely conservation biology. Conservation biology is committed solely to eliminating the negative effects of human interference with ecosystems. This field is dominated by ecologists and biologists. They employ efforts such as watershed protection, habitat restoration, and species reintroduction to remediate the damage caused by architecture, roads, and farming, but these techniques are practically alien to most architects, engineers, and designers. Conservation biologists believe that you can't restore balance in the natural world without such practices. Building professionals not knowing about conservation ecology is a major problem.

Green building must mature beyond its current state to be effective as a tool to create sustainability. A big change would be achieved if ecological science was to become a bigger component of building design and urban planning. Currently, as in the past, biologists and ecologists are not involved with designers and planners responsible for redesigning neighborhoods and communities. This is because we were not aware of ecology until the last hundred years, and construction as a discipline is much older than that. However, the future of architecture will be as much about ecosystems and habitat restoration as conservation biology is today. If not, the damage buildings, cities, roads, and infrastructure cause in nature will not stop. If we plan to have lots of nature in the coming decades and centuries, with a continued variety of species, then one essential element about buildings has to change. We will need to shift from acting like we are not part of nature to seeing ourselves as an integral part of nature. I will also look at what keystone species are and how we can learn from them to better design cities and buildings.

As I have suggested, most buildings do not stand alone but are part of suburbs, cities, and megalopolises—the boundaryless expanses where cities and towns and suburbs have grown to the point of overlapping each other. A megalopolis functions as a single economic engine where a person's standard of living is as dependent on places as far as 500 to 1,000 miles away. The last several chapters look at where green building needs to be in 100 years. I provide some guidance and direction to understand the future of green building where the goal is vast wildernesses and megacities, or globalized, intertwined societies and localized sustainability. In Chapters 10 and 11, I discuss several green and eco-cities that have gotten lots of attention over the last few years. They are images of a world still disconnected from nature. They are built in places large populations are not really meant to be. Future green architecture will need to be more than just situating a building onto a site or reducing the amount of water it uses. Cities and ecosystems will need to work together to provide unique patterns of human growth and ecological wonder. I call this ecomimicry— where civilization functions as if it is a habitat. Such a society would strengthen the ecological services that nature already provides, such as how it naturally cleans water and sequesters carbon. An amazing world awaits, full of, potentially, a century's worth of discovery and exploration in bringing green building into every built object in our human world and, at the same time, bringing the creation of buildings, roads, and other development into alignment with nature. But first, let's start with the question of what a building is today. Chapter 1 is about a new way of thinking about buildings in general while Chapter 2 is about where green building is today.

CHAPTER 1

WHEN BUILDINGS WENT BAD

Buildings were never meant to make you sick. Shelter is an essential element for survival. You can live a couple of days without water, and even longer without food, but one night exposed to rain or cold could spell your demise. Building a primitive hut such as a lean-to increases your chance of survival by almost 100 percent. The fact that buildings are no longer safe for people is at odds with our very survival.

So when did buildings become so deadly? Archaeological studies found that tribal people in Mesoamerica deforested vast areas of woodlands to build dwellings in the southwest of the United States. The logging of these forests caused topsoil to erode, and the forests never came back even hundreds of years after the natives had left. For example, the ancient Pueblo peoples known as the Anasazi built extensive complex structures in the remote deserts of northwestern New Mexico.[1] These settlements required cutting down most of the trees within the area, which damaged the Anasazi's ability to produce food from agriculture because of the loss of topsoil. The drought-stricken area has never rebounded from the deforestation and environmental degradation caused by the Anasazi, though their developments were abandoned more than 800 years ago.

The castles, churches, and cathedrals of Europe are seen as monuments of a golden age, but extravagant numbers of trees and stones were needed to complete each one. Once these edifices were built, it took mountains

Figure 1   Examples of centuries-old buildings in Europe. Credit: Neil Chambers

of logs to heat them during the winter. Burning wood in structures with bad ventilation such as those built in Europe can cause respiratory problems that lead to worse diseases like cancer and chronic bronchitis. The Environmental Protection Agency (EPA) considers inhalation of beyond a certain level of wood smoke to be unhealthy because it contains nitrogen oxides, carbon monoxide, organic gases, and fine particles. Until the twentieth century, ventilation was not a priority for architecture, nor were other means of heating available besides wood and other organic materials such as coal. So it is difficult to say when buildings went bad.

Even more modern structures like the Empire State Building were poorly built. At the time of its completion in 1931, it was considered a marvel of innovation. In 2009, plans were unveiled to update the skyscraper to be green at a cost 22 times the original price tag. The decision for such a radical renovation was seen by green building professionals and advocates as a true victory for their industry. But it also shows just how badly the building was originally constructed not even a century ago. Before modern chemicals were available for preserving wood, people used kerosene, which is highly flammable and very toxic. Lead-based paint was used until the 1970s in the United States and still coats the interiors of many older buildings. Asbestos, which had been used since 100 B.C. by the Greeks as a fire retardant, is known to cause cancer. All of these chemicals can still be found in the Empire State Building—where thousands of people go to work each day, and more than 2 million people visit each year.

Both lead paint and asbestos are now outlawed in the United States. But today many other materials and chemicals that are standard in the building industry should give us pause.[2]

HOW THE BUILDING INDUSTRY LEARNED TO POISON US

The building industry is not always easy to understand. One way to look at it is that it is like the Wild West, where two factors reign supreme: money and speed. Everyone in the building profession, from real estate developers to architects and designers, wants to keep construction costs as low as possible, and thus they always pick the cheapest materials for a job. The problem with the cheapest building materials is they are often the most toxic and lowest quality. They result in the biggest profits for the developer, but they also hold the highest potential for making anyone using a building sick.

Companies manufacturing the materials used in buildings understand that they can stay competitive only if they can offer their products at, or below, the current price of common products. They also know that they must mass-produce their materials to keep down production costs. The end result is that cheap, low-quality materials with unacceptable toxicity levels are the standard, even in so-called luxury items.

Those of us who don't work in the building industry have become so accustomed to the toxicity levels of common household materials that we overlook obvious signs that something is wrong. The woozy feeling you get from being inside a newly painted room is because a category of toxins called volatile organic compounds (also known as VOCs) are off-gassing. Paints containing VOCs are the standard for 99.9 percent of all paint jobs throughout the world. Anyone who has ever spent time in a newly painted room or hallway has inhaled VOCs. These toxins can cause eye, nose, and throat irritation along with headaches, loss of coordination, and nausea. Long-term exposure can lead to damage to your liver, kidneys, and central nervous system. Some VOCs can cause cancer. Symptoms of exposure include nose and throat discomfort, skin irritation, fatigue, and dizziness. Only in the last three to four years have paint industry giants such as Sherwin-Williams and Benjamin Moore begun to offer low-VOC (the still toxic but not as toxic option) and zero-VOC alternatives to consumers.

But simply picking a different paint will not let you avoid the toxicity conventional buildings contain. Carpets, hardwood floors, molding, wallpaper, floor tiles, floor sealants, and adhesives are packed full of hazardous chemicals. Urea-formaldehyde is a toxin commonly used in fiberboards, particleboard, and plywood—all of which are always used in building projects. Urea-formaldehyde is one of the most cost-effective ways to give wood products their flat form and makes the wood scratch resistant.

But it can also trigger asthma attacks as well as cause eye, nose, and throat irritation, wheezing and coughing, skin rashes, and severe allergic reactions, and it has been shown to cause cancer in laboratory testing. Nearly every wood product in the world uses it. You can find it in the furniture you buy and the clothes you wear. The wood used within a couch is full of urea-formaldehyde while the cushions are full of other VOCs. Bed mattresses and frames are full of these things too. Most bed linen is laden with toxins left over from the processing of the fabric. According to the EPA, studies have found that levels of several VOCs are on average two to five times higher indoors than outdoors, and after such activities as new construction, painting, or paint stripping indoor levels may be a thousand times those of the normal levels found outside. These have the same health effects as the VOCs mentioned above.[3]

Urea-formaldehyde and VOCs are child's play compared to the stuff found in everyday carpeting.[4] The fibers of carpeting are made from petroleum products, and they include as many as 120 known poisonous materials. These toxins can be found in the bonding agencies, dyes, and stain-resistant treatments of the carpets. The simple act of walking across a carpet sends fibers airborne, making it extremely easy for people to inhale them. In essence, you are inhaling oil along with a long list of chemicals. Many of the chemicals are neurotoxins, which can affect the normal activities of your nervous system. Once they are inside you, it is difficult to get them out. Carpets contain a staggering amount of other chemicals such as ethyl benzene, styrene, and acetone, some of which are listed by the EPA as extremely hazardous substances. These chemicals cause hallucinations and respiratory illness in humans.

Taken together, the combination of carpeting, paints, wood, furniture, sealants, glues, and linens in our homes and workplaces reveals just how bad these places can be for our health. Sometimes when I point this out to people, their response is that no one is dropping dead from the carpet at the office. This is because the cancer-causing agents within building materials are accumulative, and most build up over time. It can take years for these poisons to work their way into the sensitive parts of your body like the lymphatic system, where they can irritate cellular structure enough to bring about tumors.

It is nearly impossible to know just how many people have been made sick from simple household products like carpet, paint, and mattresses, but it is safe to say there have been many. These toxic choices have been the materials of choice of architects and developers for decades. And yet, for all the problems the presence of carcinogens, VOCs, and other noxious substances in common building products can cause, their potential harm pales in comparison to the damage done before they ever make it to the store to be bought.

WHERE THE DAMAGE TO HEALTH AND ENVIRONMENT STARTS

The investigation of how materials affect the environment from when their raw components are harvested until they are finally delivered and installed is called a life-cycle analysis. The life-cycle analysis can be broken into four major phases: harvesting, processing, manufacturing, and installation. For example, in the harvesting phase of steel, you first have to pull iron ore out of the ground. Very often, ore is found in remote locations, requiring wide roads to be built deep into the wilderness. Iron is the most commonly used metal in the world, mainly due to its being a key ingredient for steel. Because of this, iron represents almost 95 percent of all metal used per year worldwide.[5] To get iron, you must first mine iron ore, or the rocks and minerals that yield metallic iron during extraction. Because iron and steel are the structural materials of choice for bridges, towers, naval ships, automobiles, and just about every building in the United States more than a story high—with Japan, European countries, the United States, China, and South Korea increasing consumption by about 10 percent yearly— we are increasingly complicit in the environmental degradation caused by iron extraction, delivery, processing, and manufacturing.

To get to high-quality, large deposits of iron ore, you have to remove tons of soil and rock with explosives before electric shovels can load blasted ore into trucks. By the time all the available ore has been removed from the mine, it looks more like a moonscape than someplace on Earth. Take for example, the Mount Whaleback iron ore mine, Newman, Western Australia. Mount Whaleback is the biggest open-cut iron ore mine on the continent. Iron in its raw form is the color of rust, and the Mount Whaleback is covered in a thick layer of red iron ore dust.

The geological history of Western Australia is ancient, with most of the landscape flat and never exceeding an elevation of 4,300 feet. The Mount Whaleback mine opens the land like a mini–Grand Canyon. Mining of iron, like that of most other open-mine resources, is done in a series of steps. A layer is cut into the ground, and then another and another until, like Whaleback, it resembles a huge red rock ziggurat made of terraces 50 feet deep.[6] From tip to tail, the mine is three miles long, more than a mile wide, and several hundred feet deep. The gigantic pieces of machinery necessary to move the ore are dwarfed against the human-made canyon. This is how most iron ore mines look. In the United States, Michigan has three of the six iron-rich areas.

The blasting needed to carve into the earth means removing anything living on the site along with precious topsoil. Erosion poses a significant problem as miners begin to blast and remove the iron. Environmental impacts and risks start at the very beginning of the process. For example, many valuable metals are present within iron ore that are soluble in acid. The ore will go through several stages of processing. It is typically processed close to the mining site the first time, and leaching of acidic solutions is common. The proper disposal of wastewater presents problems because of the typical remoteness of mines. The grinding of nonmetals like quarried stone and limestone pose air-pollution problems as airborne particulates are released. Solid waste like soil, waste rock, and vegetation overburden the general area. Toxic fumes from solvents and vapors from heavy equipment make the areas unsuitable for life. Water used for processing is contaminated with cyanide, solvents, sulfur dioxide, sulfuric acid, cyanide compounds, cresols, hydrocarbons, copper compounds and zinc dust, aluminum sulfate, lime, iron, calcium salts, and starches. Artificial ponds are constructed to retain the water from flowing away from mining sites, but often regulatory rules can't be enforced, so it escapes into the environment. Once the mine is completely depleted, the walls of the mine are unstable, topsoil is absent, and pollution is high, making recovery to a more natural condition impossible.

Hauling loads of iron from work site to factory causes large quantities of dirt to become loosened along the road. The loose dirt gets swept away during rainstorms into streams and rivers. As rainfall sweeps the earth away as runoff, it takes along with it any toxins or chemicals such as grease, gasoline, motor oil, and antifreeze that may have splashed from the trucks. These impurities enter streams and water tables and are absorbed by the soil. Roads on hillsides or mountains create erosion, sometimes destroying entire hillsides over time. Unstable shoulders and roadways will supply hefty amounts of dirt into waterways like rivers and creeks in the form of erosion. This dirt becomes a primary agent that chokes riverine habitats by coating the bottom of rivers. Grasses, shrubs, and brush that stabilize riverbanks disappear due to the root systems being covered with sediment. The sedimentation that occurs clogs the foundation of essential habitat for insects that are the basis of these ecosystems' food chain. For example, the rocky bottoms of a river act as nurseries for insects like dragonflies and damselflies. Birds, fish, water beetles, frogs, spiders, lizards, and even larger species of other insects feed on dragonflies from the moment they are larvae until they are adults. Without them the web of life is off balance, soon affecting other species. A river in a forested area impacted by sedimentation from mining can become defunct, losing the natural method by which the water flowing within it is cleaned.

The unforeseen side effect of rivers becoming defunct is that flooding increases. When the natural habitat is fully intact, the velocity and volume of water are modulated by variations in depth as well as width. Also, vegetation and the way rivers wind create ecological checks and balances to control any sudden surges of water from rainfall or snowmelt. However, as riverbanks lose the grasses and brush that hold them together, the banks erode and widen. This, along with additional sedimentation, makes them shallower. Where the ecological conditions could at one time withstand a rush of excess water, now the system has been robbed of that ability.

The only place for the flow to go is over the banks and into whatever is built on the other side.

Worse still is that more water is pouring into the river than before. With all of the vegetation removed from the hillsides or watershed, there is nothing to capture and hold it throughout the landscape. Storm water flows directly into the waterbody at a faster rate and in a higher quantity. If the natural conditions were still intact, less runoff would make it to the stream or river because layers of leaves, root systems, depressions, holes, and other characteristics of the ground would soak it up as it moved across the landscape. Without these things, the water is unimpeded, resulting in worse and worse flooding—which, as many disasters have shown, means more damage to property, loss of jobs, and, in more and more cases, loss of lives.

Roads cut for hauling iron ore and other goods to a factory can also create massive floods in low-lying areas where towns, farms, and roads are typically located. Many people think that the raw materials we must

Figure 2 Mountaintop coal mine pit. Credit: B. Mark Schmerling

extract from the earth are a prerequisite for society, that we have to have the resources at whatever cost, monetary or environmental. The toll on humans is greatest with regard to the side effects of problems caused. You may have on occasion seen stories in the media about record-breaking rainfall followed by extensive damage to property. Homes, businesses, cars, and bridges are washed away during storms. Flooding costs companies and individuals billions of dollars every year. Most pundits do not look beyond the notion that such issues are caused by lack of tax dollars being spent to update civil underpinning like levees and dams. But the truth is that it is the damage inflected onto ecosystems across the country in the name of progress that is the deeper root of the problem.

When raw materials are extracted from the earth, it is known as the harvesting phase of the life cycle. It is the first step of turning individual natural resources into things that we will use for buildings down the road. For example, timber is harvested from a forest to be turned into plywood or other wood products. Or, iron is mined to eventually be combined with other resources to become steel. Once you have cut or extracted the raw materials, they will be delivered to a factory to begin the processing phase where they begin to be transformed into something unrecognizable from their original form.

After the iron ore has been drilled, dug, or ripped from the earth, it is combined with coke to make steel. To induce these two raw materials to fuse, a furnace is heated to temperatures of 750 to 3,200 degrees Fahrenheit. Only fossil fuels like coal, natural gas, or petroleum create the tremendous amount of energy necessary to generate such temperatures. As a result, plumes of greenhouse gases like hydrocarbons and nitrogen oxides come from steel factories along with dioxins and sulfur dioxide (which causes acid rain). Other nasty by-products from steel production include slag and fly ash. Slag is a waste product from processing iron ore. Fly ash comes from burning coal—it is one of two basic types of coal ash. Fly ash is the lighter of the two and, until scrubbers were installed on coal-plant smokestacks, would be released into the air from chimneys. Today, fly ash is removed from the smoke column and retained in an ash slurry on-site. Both slag and fly ash can be used as a substitute for Portland cement in concrete, lowering the use of energy in the highly energy-intense process of concrete production. It also means that these waste products are being reused, rather than just being stored essentially as garbage. Many green designers tout the use of such materials in their designs. But for all the positives of recycling the postindustrial sludge, the process does not remit the problems of iron mining and processing or of coal-fired power. In 2008, it became terribly clear how disruptive the by-product could be when a dike for a retention pond broke at the Kingston Fossil Plant in Kingston, Tennessee, about 140 miles east of Nashville. The rupture released 1.1 billion gallons of coal fly ash slurry, devastating 300 acres of the surrounding land, damaging homes, and flowing into the Emory River and Clinch River, tributaries of the Tennessee. It was the largest accidental release of coal fly ash in US history. Inside slurry, along with fly ash, are heavy metals such as lead—known to cause birth defects and learning disabilities in toddlers—left over from the manufacturing process that often escapes into waterways and into the air. They slowly find their way into the water table and then into creeks, streams, lakes, and rivers until they find their way to the cups of water we drink, or into the food we eat. (The mercury found in fish is also a by-product of the production of steel.)

These are the environmental risks of building materials during the first three phases of the materials life cycle. After these initial steps comes installation, when, if the materials are toxic, you get to inhale them when they off-gas. Because harvesting, processing, and manufacturing are typically far from each other, and then the final site is additional mileage, a product you buy could have traveled nearly 20,000 miles during the process from cradle to your living room or work space. Scraps and demolition waste from construction materials represent a large percentage of the waste stream. An estimated 40 percent of all waste comes from construction. In 2003, the EPA calculated roughly 164 million tons of construction and demolition from buildings were generated in the United States annually.[7] Durability plays a part in how long you use the product. If,

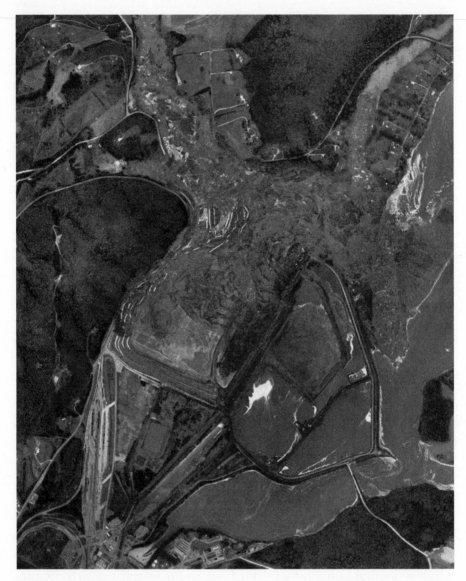

Figure 3 Aerial view of one of the worst fly ash disasters in history. Credit: Tennessee Valley Authority

for example, the carpeting or furniture is of bad quality, that means it will be discarded more often than better-constructed products.

Today, due to regulation, the steel industry may have left the United States, but the pollution is still being generated elsewhere. What Americans learned about pollution has yet to be learned by the countries that took in the orphaned companies. And for all the good the regulation and enforcement did in the United States, the manufacturing process still results in clouds of toxic fumes blowing back to us. For years, NASA has recorded smog traveling across the Pacific Ocean reaching California, Nevada, and Oregon as large masses, and some clouds make it as far east as North and South Dakota and into the Great Plains.

The story of steel is a typical story, not the exception. Fast and cheap buildings are erasing vast tracks of wilderness. Species and ecosystems are destroyed and floodwaters polluted with heavy metals, and chemical spills are leaching onto croplands and into urban areas. Millions of dollars are lost to natural disasters that are actually caused by the production of building materials. And once the products and materials are installed into offices, homes, churches, and stores, they poison us for years.

Buildings are not just homes, offices, and churches—they are also all the steps it takes to get the building materials to the site and installed. Buildings are just as much the plumes·of smoke exhausted during the forging of steel as they are structures with doors and windows. When you add the energy needed to make all building materials along with the energy buildings use throughout their lifetime, the total represents roughly 75 percent of all the energy generated in the world. Buildings are the source of more greenhouse gases like carbon dioxide and carbon monoxide than any other industry on the planet—more than cars, airplanes, trucks, and boats combined. They are the tons and tons of chemicals that go into breaking down wood chips into pulp, and the tons and tons of fossil fuels burned to create aluminum, steel, and concrete.[8] They are the mercury you find in fish, and the lead you find in rivers. And they are the places we go home to, only to be exposed to off-gassing of VOCs and urea-formaldehyde.

This is not what anyone wants when they build a building.

CHAPTER 2

THE HISTORY OF GREEN BUILDING

If buildings have been around for thousands of years, green building is comparatively new. It first gained attention in the midst of the 1973 energy crisis. People sat for hours in their cars waiting in long lines for gasoline. Prices were at an all-time high. Public morale was low. Jimmy Carter, the president of the United States at that time, installed solar panels on the White House to show that alternatives to oil existed. Initially developed by NASA to power spaceships, solar power technology had been around since the 1950s, but because it was wildly expensive and thus impractical to implement, it was never widely used for buildings. President Carter also suggested other ways to save energy, such as putting on a sweater when at home instead of turning up the heat. For a short time the country followed his suggestions, though when the crisis was over and energy prices returned to normal, the knitwear came off and the heat was turned back up. Still, a generation of engineers and thinkers had been changed. They could see a future in saving energy—and that it could be good business.

Their first target was the heating, ventilation, and air-conditioning equipment in residential and commercial buildings. The energy used within these units accounts for 80 percent of the energy used overall in a building. Through tinkering, engineers discovered that performance was improved when they used higher-quality parts for motors, gears, and fan belts as well as improved fan speeds. The retooling of existing models showed a jump in efficiency between 10 and 20 percent. Engineers also learned that making walls and windows more airtight had a direct effect on reducing the amount of energy needed to regulate temperatures inside a home or office. With the simple act of plugging gaps in walls and doubling the insulation around windows and doors, an additional savings of 5 to 10 percent was found. New green buildings combining these improvements were already showing savings upward of 25 to 30 percent.

After the low-hanging fruit was picked, progress became much slower. But energy savings had begun to catch on, and an increasing number of architects and engineers wanted to incorporate renewable energy technologies, particularly solar panels, into their buildings. But solar panels had to compete against standard forms of energy, typically those from fossil fuels, the price of which the energy industry keeps low by mass production. This made it very difficult for small energy companies to enter the market, or for just about any building to financially justify using solar panels as an energy source. Pound for pound, coal and other fossil fuels generate 100 times more electricity than renewable energies. From the 1970s to 2001, solar panel projects grew sluggishly throughout the United States.

It was only in 1988 that the myth that green buildings were always too expensive began to be dismantled. That year, the headquarters of the Natural Resources Defense Council, in New York City, was the first widely recognized green building to employ energy-conserving technologies that saved more than 30 percent on energy compared to conventional construction, while the cost of construction was not much higher than that of conventional construction.[1] Designed by Randy Croxton, the project brought together low-toxic materials with energy-saving techniques like daylighting and open floor plans that dramatically cut electricity consumption. This building is today still a strong example of how green buildings improve the quality of a work space as well as save businesses energy and money.

In 1992, the Energy Policy Act (EPAct) passed by the US Congress mandated performance levels for energy and water within buildings.

Mandated energy and water performance are pretty much the same thing, in that fixtures and equipment are designed and manufactured to use less resources than conventional products on the market. For example, water fixtures like toilets would use only one gallon per flush versus the two to three gallons that some models have been made to use in the past. Other mandatory performance criteria include the amount of water flowing from faucets or showerheads per minute. This legislation put an end to any arguments that cheap and fast should outweigh the need for efficient, safe, and green. States were required to adopt energy standards for every imaginable aspect of buildings.

The EPAct also ushered in the Energy Star program, which rates the efficiency of everything from flat-screen televisions to laptops to microwaves, fans, lighting fixtures, dishwashers, washing machines, and printers. When a product has the logo, it signifies that it uses less energy than other similar products. These standards allow consumers to make informed purchases without understanding the technical aspects of energy consumption.

Another substantial event occurred in June of 1992 when the United Nations held the Earth Summit in Rio de Janeiro, Brazil. The event was a lightning rod for establishing a global consensus on how best to protect the planet, and involved experts in chemistry, urban design, biology, mining, and other fields, as well as government officials. The Earth Summit prompted a group of design and real estate professionals in the United States to draft guidelines entitled Leadership in Energy and Environmental Design, or LEED, that would be used to rate how green any given project really was. The LEED system has been used to rate thousands of buildings since it was first launched in 1998. Local, state, and federal legislation has been created based on it. Corporations and small businesses alike recognize a LEED rating as a stamp of quality assurance that they are doing the right thing for the earth.

GREEN BUILDING TODAY

Today, the five most important issues in green building are reducing the amount of energy buildings consume, changing the types of energy

Figure 4   Sign from the Dust Bowl era in the United States. Credit: Library of Congress

buildings use, improving the types of materials used for construction, eliminating practices that waste water, and mitigating problems with indoor air quality.

In popular culture, energy is the topic of most debate when discussing sustainability. However, it is water that has always been of paramount importance within buildings and nations. The Romans built aqueducts to bring freshwater into the center of cities to compensate for the increased consumption in urban areas. Indeed, by definition water infrastructure projects are undertaken when human populations overconsume, or promise to overconsume, local supplies. Throughout history, various regions of the United States have faced water shortages. The Dust Bowl of the 1930s was the result of prolonged droughts throughout the prairies of the Great Plains and Canada. The huge clouds of dried dirt that swept across the land were caused by decades of extensive farming without crop rotation, fallow fields, cover crops, or other techniques to prevent erosion.[2]

Plowing techniques through the grasslands of the prairies' virgin topsoil had displaced the natural vegetation that keeps soil from eroding and that traps moisture during dry periods and high winds.

In 2007 and 2008, the Southeastern United States experienced widespread shortages. A study from Columbia University determined the droughts were not unprecedented in severity but what the researchers called a "typical event."[3] The lack came from overpopulation throughout the region. For example, during the 17 years between 1990 and 2007, the population of Georgia increased nearly 50 percent, to 9.5 million. Most of the growth occurred around Atlanta. The human explosion along with lack of rain put tremendous pressure on the Lake Lanier Reservoir, Atlanta's main water supply. The lake's water level shrank to historic lows, and the crisis created tension between environmentalists and political leaders within the state and with bordering states. The water needed in Georgia was just as needed in neighboring states of Florida and Alabama. Because Atlanta was overpopulated to the point that sharing resources could potentially cause massive shortages, they opted to restrict others from accessing reservoirs. This led to a full-blown water war involving the states of Georgia, Florida, and Alabama. Randy Serraglio, conservation advocate at the Center for Biological Diversity, explained that "this is what happens when you have a dramatically increasing population relying on the same limited supply of water. Unfortunately, it is usually other species that pay the price for our inability to responsibly manage growth and consumption." To make matters worse, Atlanta is projected to double its water demand over the next 30 years. In 2009, a federal judge ruled that Atlanta would have to find another source of water besides the reservoir, observing that state and local governments support growth because it increases tax revenue yet do not consider the long-term consequences of unchecked growth and plan accordingly for the necessary resources infrastructure. He went on to say that individual citizens do not consider "frequently enough their consumption of our scarce resources, absent a crisis situation."[4]

Scarcity of water is projected to affect as many as 36 states by 2013, according to US government estimates. California consumes nearly one-sixth of all water within the United States. Global warming could cause 14 states to face an extreme risk of limitations on water availability by 2050, according to an analysis by consulting firm Tetra Tech for the Natural Resources Defense Council.[5]

Against this backdrop, when the EPAct was created, it mandated that water fixtures such as toilets, faucets, and other appliances that use water must reduce consumption. As the law came into effect, many companies created unique options for consumers that eventually fostered a second program by the EPA called WaterSense, which rates the amount of water bathroom and kitchen fixtures used. For example, if a toilet used less water per flush than others, it would be awarded the WaterSense label. When a building uses only products bearing the Energy Star and WaterSense labels, it can reduce energy consumption by 20 to 30 percent and water consumption by more than 60 percent.

Starting in the 1990s, green buildings began to incorporate several easy ways to reduce water usage. One was to eliminate the irrigation of lawns and other types of landscaping, which can account for 25 to 30 percent of the water a building uses. The most common way to do this is through the landscape and gardening approach called xeriscaping, which emphasizes the use of drought-tolerant native species that are adapted to the variations of local climates. Water usage reductions can also be achieved in indoor plumbing. After installing a dual-flush toilet, for example, a user can choose how much water is needed per flush. As much as half a gallon or more can be saved each flush this way.

Even more innovative are fixtures such as waterless urinals that do not need any water. Such products are growing in popularity as well-known makers of water fixtures like Kohler develop lines for the home market, and lesser known makers such as Waterless, Falcon, and ZeroFlush have introduced their own lines of waterless urinals to compete for clients. Waterless urinals have many benefits. Because no water is used for flushing, they save owners money in utility bills. Waterless urinals have far fewer parts than conventional urinals, so they malfunction less often and are less expensive to maintain. They are equipped with a deodorizing

Figure 5 Low-flow bathroom fixtures save water by using less water during every flush. Credit: Neil Chambers

liquid that acts as a sanitation and smell barrier, promoting a safe, odor-free bathroom environment. When a conventional urinal is flushed, it releases an aerosol of water droplets containing bacteria and microbes. Once this microscopic cloud is shot into the air, it can be inhaled or ingested.

Gray-water systems—which take so-called dirty water from sinks, showers, fountains, and dishwashers, and reuse it for nonpotable (non-drinkable) purposes in locations such as toilets—are also becoming popular. Black-water systems take water from the same sources as gray-water systems and from water including human waste. These systems then filter, treat, and reuse the water for irrigation, or it goes back into nonpotable use to start the process all over again. Both gray-water and black-water systems are hygienic and safe for residential and commercial use. Companies like General Electric have developed technologies such as black-water filtration devices that can be used in buildings to purify and treat wastewater coming from manufacturing processes or that has been contaminated by human sewage. The application of a full black-water system means that pretty much all of the water that comes into a building can be reused.

Likewise, architects today have a wide range of strategies and design methods available to implement such things as energy efficiency in green buildings. For example, a popular alternative today to wasteful incandescent lightbulbs are compact fluorescent lightbulbs, or CFLs. CFLs use about 10 to 30 percent less energy than incandescents. They cost a little more than standard lightbulbs, but they also last longer, about five to seven years longer. Many offices are installing motion sensors to turn off lights when no one is in a room, or daylight dimmers for offices. Another example of energy efficiency is replacing old windows with up-to-date windows with low-e glass. Low-e glass is a type of glass with a film applied that helps reduce the amount of heat that escapes through it during cold seasons or penetrates it in warm seasons.

After their sluggish start in the twentieth century, solar panel projects now enjoy federal tax incentives, driving down the cost sharply and spurring on other renewable energies. Commercially available solar cells are commonly 12 to 15 percent efficient, a fourfold increase over those of only a few years ago.[6] This means that the panels can convert about 15 percent of the energy from the sun into electricity.

Solar panels are used in two ways; one is called solar thermal. Solar thermal for homes is used to preheat domestic water for things like showering and washing dishes. At a large scale, the sun heats water or another fluid to drive turbines or other machinery to create electricity. The other type of solar panel is photovoltaic, or PV, which produces electricity directly from the sun without moving parts. A type of PV called single-crystal can reach between 20 and 30 percent efficiency. Other examples of renewable energy in use today include wind, tidal, geothermal, and bioenergy.

Of course, building materials are also of tremendous interest to design professionals involved with green projects. For a material to be green it has to be made from recycled, reused, or renewable materials. Recycled content comes in two major forms. One is as postconsumer waste. These are materials that households or businesses use and then discard. Many paper products contain postconsumer waste. The other type is pre-consumer waste, meaning that the material is diverted from a manufacturing process or industrial practices. An example of pre-consumer waste is the fly ash created by coal burning. Both post- and pre-consumer waste are collected, reprocessed, and made into new products.

Reused products are salvaged goods used again for the same purpose they were originally produced. Antiques are a good example of reused products. They may be refinished or repaired, but they are essentially the same item.

A renewable material is made from something that is easily replaced by nature in a short period of time. Renewable building materials are those that take no more than five years to replenish. Renewable materials must also be harvested, processed, and manufactured within 500 miles of their final destination. And, of course, they should have little or no hazardous or toxic materials. Common examples of renewable materials include bamboo, linoleum, and cork, which are used as flooring, as well as wool, which is used to make carpeting. Agrifiber products are another

Figure 6 On-site solar panel installations are a more environmentally sound method for using alternative energy sources. Credit: US Fish and Wildlife Service

renewable material. They are derived from agricultural waste and can be used to make boards that do not use any toxic chemicals and result in zero off-gassing after they are installed. They are a perfect alternative to plywood and particleboard laden with harmful substances.

Green materials like agrifiber are important because they replace wood products made from hardwood and rainforest trees. Trees are the lifeblood of many ecosystems, and removing them can destroy habitat for countless species. Hardwoods like cherry and oak take many years to mature, which makes it tough for ecosystems to recover once the trees have been removed. The United States is the largest importer of tropical hardwoods. Mahogany from South America and Africa along with Ipe and Jatoba from Brazil are commonly used for furniture, doors, boardwalks, decking, plywood, and flooring. Trees from southeast Asian rainforests are used for paneling, cabinets, subflooring, and doors. These important trees are so overharvested that they are even used unnecessarily in the manufacture of things like bathroom plunger handles and pencils.[7]

Other common materials that have a tremendous environmental impact are stone products like granite, slate, marble, and limestone, which are used in high volumes for interiors to make countertops, stairs, hearths, and tables. Excavating granite from the ground requires thousands of gallons of water—the runoff is a source of sediment and toxins into rivers and streams. An entire market of green products has been developed to replace them. Green building design looks to find better materials and methods to create countertops. A popular example comes from companies that reprocess glass and concrete to create eye-catching surfaces for cafés, restaurants, homes, and retail stores. Another ingenious alternative to granite are countertops made from 100 percent recycled paper. The material is compressed into large one- to two-inch-thick sheets that are as hard as rock. The paper can be dyed with an assortment of colors while also being a highly durable surface. Such products are made from paper that has been saturated with nontoxic, VOC-free resins. The resin bath creates a nonporous surface that provides a lifetime of stain and water resistance. And like more rocky countertops, when the surface is cut or marked, these countertops can be refinished to retain their new looks. The material can also be used for furniture, vertical panels and partitions, signs, and cutlery handles. For use in countertops, such recycled surfaces rival the strength of quarried stone. And because the products use recycled materials, they remove things like glass and concrete from the waste stream by putting them to work in new items.

Precast concrete countertops are another option for using recycled content. A good precast company with green principles can customize all countertops to meet the sustainable requirements of a project. Local businesses typically use materials manufactured locally. The concrete can contain recycled glass, metals, porcelain, and other aggregate to increase levels to as high as 75 to 80 percent recycled content. And manufacturers treat all of their surfaces with VOC-free sealers. All of the green countertop materials available are always more attractive, versatile, and adaptive than conventional stone materials. Their harvesting does not require mining, and they are often developed by companies with a sustainability mindset, so they are thinking about how they can create healthier products from the very beginning.

Countertops are really just the tip of the iceberg for green materials. Every toxic, harmful building material has an alternative. Most major metropolitan areas now provide ample access to green materials suppliers. This is important because the more options consumers have, the more green buildings there will be.

WHAT'S NEXT?—LIFE-CYCLE ANALYSIS

Innovative materials are entering the market at a breakneck pace. Entire markets like cleantech and greentech are forming to cater to the needs of building energy savings. Renewable energy technologies are also growing. In 2009, more renewable energy than any other type was installed throughout the world. Every year, the percentage of renewable energy generated in the United States grows. Water technologies are also growing in popularity and ease of access. Gray-water systems are often a standard practice in geographic locations where there is little water from local sources, such as Las Vegas and Phoenix.

But there are blind spots within the current green building industry and the sustainability movement as a whole. The EPAct gives direction to solve surface-level problems with technologies like energy-saving devices, but the concern over energy consumption overshadows addressing the troubles that are only getting worse in the natural world. Habitat is disappearing at an alarming rate. Species are at the brink of extinction. Water quality issues are alarming as well. The US Environmental Protection Agency's 2000 National Water Quality Inventory assessed the nation's rivers, streams, lake, ponds, estuaries, and Great Lakes and found that between 39 and 78 percent of the water bodies tested did not support the water quality standards and were designated as impaired. More than 75 percent of the Great Lakes shoreline miles and over 50 percent of assessed estuarine square miles did not meet water quality standards.[8]

If people do not pay attention to the impact buildings are having on the environment, then even if all buildings in the future are green by today's definition, the problems that building construction and use are creating within nature will not go away. Energy-efficient lightbulbs are great for saving energy and making your power bill less, but they do not grow back forests.

This is where the importance of the life-cycle analysis comes in. Life-cycle analysis is not standard practice by any of the design, construction, or real estate professions, green or otherwise. Currently, it is virtually impossible to know exactly how much damage is being caused to the environment by buildings because the companies that create the products that have traditionally gone into buildings do not release information about their processes. To know the process is to know how much energy, chemicals, and water are used to make a product. This type of information allows a consumer a more realistic appraisal of a product. If you knew that VOCs were in a paint or urea-formaldehyde had been used to make a mattress, you could decide if you wanted the product or not. Likewise, life cycle shows you where materials originate. Many products have labels stating that they are made in America or made in Taiwan, but that tells you only where the product was assembled. The materials used in a simple product like a lamp or bookshelf can be harvested in one country, sent to another country to be processed, then shipped to two or three other nations for manufacturing before they end up in the product in a store with a price tag on it. Each step takes energy and results in carbon emissions and pollution. When you known just how much a product affects the environment, you may decide to pick a different option.

Life-cycle analysis needs to become a standard approach for everything we buy. In the same way, a nutrition menu provides insight to the ingredients of what you are eating. For example, it lists things like high-fructose corn syrup and saturated fats. If you do not mind eating these things, you are able to make that decision with the facts in front of you. If you do not want to eat those types of ingredients, you also get to make a decision to not eat them. The same is true for life-cycle analysis. Labeling systems should be required on all product packaging or available online and be as commonplace as ingredients and labels are for foods. Until life-cycle analysis is an essential part of designing buildings, not enough attention will be given to the environmental damage that so many common building materials and practices are responsible for. In truth, many of today's so-called green materials are only slightly better than their conventional counterparts. For example, the manufacturing of low-e glass has the same ecological impact as that of standard glass. Energy Star appliances are not currently evaluated on the amount of pollution that was caused in their processing or manufacturing. Thus, there is still much room for improvement. Moreover, there is no way for ordinary people to actively engage in life-cycle analysis. It is a difficult practice for most designers and engineers to understand. This runs the risk of companies and designers providing so-called green products or materials that are labeled as such based on narrow criteria, and it overlooks the bigger picture.

Buildings are not just buildings. They are interconnected with the larger dynamic of ecological impact from the manufacturing and processing of materials, the transportation of those materials and products to and from factories, and ultimately to their installation in homes and offices. And for the most part that is where green building today stops. It only tries to solve the problem of individual buildings. It does not take into consideration the bigger problems caused by the pollution and contamination that go into making building materials. It also does not take into account the damage caused by the infrastructure that makes the building possible in the first place. For example, a building is not of much use if the lights do not work or you can't flush a toilet. So the building is as much a part of the plumbing that brings the water to it as it is the manufacturing of the materials that go into building it. Likewise, transportation infrastructure like highways and streets allows workers to get to their business each day and back home again each night. Infrastructure is never built to feed just one home or office building; it connects all types of buildings, from residential to commercial, educational, religious, cultural, and governmental. Without these vast networks of pipes, roads, and wiring, few buildings could be built. In effect, the infrastructure that supports buildings is just as much a part of our buildings as are their materials and the processes used in their manufacture.

This makes the view of a building much more expansive. We cannot fix the problems of buildings by simply dealing with individual buildings. We have to look at the problem from the perspective of cities, towns, regions, and, eventually, nations and multiple nations. Creating green buildings by today's measure helps, but it doesn't go far toward addressing our many critical problems with infrastructure, particularly energy and water.

CHAPTER 3

HOW INFRASTRUCTURE MAKES
WATER WORK FOR US

Any report on resource usage in the United States will state that agriculture is the number one consumer of water, but that is only partially true and comes from a very limited view of how buildings impact the environment. The actual single largest consumer of water is buildings. Overall, they use about twice as much as agricultural production. A national breakdown of water usage shows 40 percent going to agricultural irrigation, with another 39 percent going to thermoelectric power, 13 percent to residential and commercial buildings, 5 percent to manufacturing, and about 1 percent each to livestock and mining.[1] But these percentages overlook how much of each category of usage is ultimately geared toward providing architecture with energy, materials, services, and, of course, water. For example, of the water used in thermoelectricity production, almost 70 percent of it on average will be devoured by individual structures for their operations. Likewise, most of the manufacturing in the United States involves building products, so a high percentage of the water used in US manufacturing should also be considered water for buildings. Much of the mining is directly or indirectly undertaken for the manufacturing and processing of materials that ultimately end up in buildings. Only the 13 percent for residential and commercial buildings (referred to as public supply) is

Figure 7   Livestock contribute to climate change. Credit: USDA

counted as water used for architecture. Truth be told, buildings contribute to between 50 and 60 percent of all water that is used in America.

As discussed in Chapter 2, shortages are seen as a product of overexcited growth of local areas, but singling out people as the cause is not as correct as it may seem. The US Department of Homeland Security recommends storing one gallon of safe, clean, purified water per day per person in a family for emergencies like earthquakes. For everyday uses, people can do anything necessary with between 15 and 25 gallons a day such as for drinking, food preparation, and bathing. The average American uses more than five times that. Simply showing categories along with the percentages of water being used is not the entire story. Buildings are allowed to use more water than necessary, and the systems that support that use are geared toward providing an endless supply. The buildings of today are designed and equipped with ample abilities to waste water. Without a norm for customers to pick products with less life-cycle impact, we can't expect people to be able to discern between water-intense products and water-conserving products. Some blame can be put on the architects, engineers, and real estate developers, as well as the manufacturers of the building materials themselves, for focusing on profits over human safety and the health of the environment. But they are not acting in a vacuum. The larger reason how and why buildings are so wasteful has to do with a much more basic component of how societies are built.

THE IMPORTANCE OF INFRASTRUCTURE

Nothing works without infrastructure. It ties us together in ways we do not normally see. But what is it? To answer that, imagine you are standing at a factory in Pennsylvania that produces steel. How does it make the steel? I don't mean the process of combining iron and coke in a superhot furnace, but a more basic step. How does all the stuff that goes into making steel get there? The iron ore did not just appear in the factory; it had to come from somewhere else. So did the coke. If you were standing outside of the factory, you would see trucks and trains coming and going all day delivering loads of the two goods. Once they are on the property, how do they get into the superhot furnace? The iron ore and coke don't just combine themselves. Someone has to set up the furnace and put the stuff in it. All of the equipment needed to combine the two substances had to get there too. In modern factories, often the process is automated, but a few people are still needed to run the automation. These employees don't live in the steel mill. They are coming from their own homes and apartments in other places by car, truck, or motorcycle. How did they get there? More importantly, if no one could get to the factory, would any steel get produced? If you can't get to work, someone else will do the work. If no one can get to work, the work can't get done.

The matrix of roads, highways, and railways are the backbone of transportation infrastructure that lets the employees and materials get to the plant. Imagine you work in an office park outside of Houston. You use the transportation infrastructure to get to work just like the steelworker in Pennsylvania and just about everyone else in the country used it to get to work. After a few hours on the job, you need to take a break and go to the bathroom to wash your hands. You get up from your desk, walk down the hall, and go into the restroom. The lights are off, so you flip a switch and in less than a moment the bathroom is bright. You go over to the sink and turn on the faucet to wash your hands. Water begins to flow. A couple of pumps from the soap dispenser, a little hand-wringing, some lather, and—within seconds—clean hands. It is as if the water and energy were just waiting for you to use it. But how did the water come out of the faucet? It is the magic of infrastructure—literally, thousands of miles of wiring, cable, piping, conduit, canals, power plants, transmission lines, and a list of thousands of other things that make it possible.

Neither buildings nor people in the modern world can function without infrastructure. It is the framework and foundation that allows everything to happen. It is the massive network of roads, highways, water supply, air travel, sewer systems, power and energy grids, and telecommunications that provides the services that allow our daily lives to go about as they do. It is power plants, satellites, power lines, pipes, conduits, roads, asphalt, tunnels, gas lines, bridges, railways, airports, and fiber optics. We interact with it and hardly ever notice.

When you are driving down a street, you are interfacing with the transportation infrastructure. If the road stops, you stop. If the road turns right, you turn right. It determines where you go. Flush a toilet, use a water fountain, or start a garden hose, and you are engaging with an enormous labyrinth of pipes, dams, reservoirs, filtration plants, pumps, and channels that allows water to work for us. The same is true for every time you use electricity or natural gas. You are interacting with a vast system of wires, conduits, power plants, refinery stations, power lines, and mechanisms that make up what is called the energy grid.

Buildings are an extension of infrastructure. Take away infrastructure, and your buildings will stop functioning. It is such a part of daily life that it is easy to forget that it is there. Literally, because the majority of the pipes, conduits, and wiring that make up infrastructure are buried underground.

I have heard people talk about how we are connected by some unseen force that is all knowing and determines where we go in life. For a long time I thought they were talking about God. As I gained experience within the building world, I realized they were actually talking about infrastructure.

HOW WATER WORKS

Water is the source of life. Over the course of billions of years of evolution on Earth, plants and animals first developed within the depths of oceans, and then in lakes, streams, and creeks. Life found land after populating the seas and tributaries. For aeons, people have built civilizations around making water work for them. Across Europe from Istanbul to Rome, the aqueducts the Romans built, as noted in Chapter 2, brought clean, crisp water into the cities of the ancient empire. The people of antiquity constructed bathhouses and fountains at the points the water reached and entered settlements and villages. Fresh clean water kept the Romans healthy and allowed them to build their empire. The native people of Mesoamerica, like the ancestors of the Hopi Indians in the American Southwest, carved aqueducts into the ground to supply water to crops. Until the advent of engines, motors, trains, and roads, people used the natural currents of rivers and oceans to move goods, to establish communities, and to connect people in the same way we use highways today. Water is as much a part of human history as buildings. When it rains and water is plentiful, societies are strong. As soon as it starts running dry, problems start to happen.

Water is engineered today basically the same way it was in Roman times. The fundamental law of water is that it runs downhill in the path of least resistance. You can tap a lake or river to carry water as far as you want as long as it goes downhill. It is a beautiful thing. If a lake is at the top of a mountain, it can service everyone below it without the use of a single pump. You do not even need pumps to get water up into tall buildings. Water's natural pressure can feed it up some 20 to 25 stories before assistance is needed. And supplying a populace with clean, fresh water for drinking, washing clothes, and brushing teeth helps to maintain adequate hygiene and health and to ward off waterborne diseases like cholera and typhoid.

It is one thing to bring clean water in, but you have to be just as vigilant about getting soiled, dirty water out. Can you imagine the problems from having as much clean water as you wanted but being able to flush your toilet only once a week? Sewage systems are designed to accommodate the water that comes out of a building or a city—that is, the same amount or more than goes in—as well as to carry storm water from an area. Infrastructure is expensive and takes a long time to construct, too, so when a civil project is undertaken, engineers usually design systems for future capacity and peak loads. For example, research by Thames Water, the utility that operates London's water supply, has found that spikes in usage happen just after dark during Ramadan and at halftime of World Cup soccer games.[2] So if a heavy rain is happening at the same time as the whistle for the midgame break is blown, the system has to be able to deal with the influx of wastewater. If it is not, you get raw sewage in the streets—something engineers do not want to happen. In a house or office, inexpensive plastic piping can be used for plumbing fixtures, but for the larger pipes needed in city- or region-wide infrastructure you must use iron pipes or concrete conduits to withstand the pressure of all the water running through them.

Once the water is taken away from the general area of collection, it has to be treated. This entails a long list of chemicals and processes that reads more like a way to pollute water than to clean it. Conventional wastewater treatment systems are not designed to produce usable end products.[3] Sewage systems used in storm water management to take runoff from urban areas are called combined sewage systems (or CSS). When these systems are over capacity, they dump raw sewage into rivers and lakes. Combined sewer systems are remnants of the country's early infrastructure and so are typically found in older communities. Roughly 772 communities containing about 40 million people located throughout the Northeast, the Great Lakes region, and the Pacific Northwest use such systems.[4]

Even after wastewater is treated, it is still fairly toxic to people and ecologies. For discharge from treatment plants to be benign to nature and aquatic animals, water typically needs to go through three or four additional steps of purification. Americans have access to a full and extensive system of water delivery and extraction. It is so extensive it allows the people of the United States to use over 408 million gallons of water[5] every day from sources like rivers and other surface sources.[6] This is enough water to empty out the Great Lakes every 48 years.[7]

The majority of the water systems throughout the United States were built during the 30 years after the Second World War. The engineers knew that the cheapest and fastest way to get water to thirsty people was to make conduits huge as well as permanent. No one ever wants to be short of water. So they dug deep holes and placed iron pipes and concrete tunnels into the ground. The engineers who built the waterworks infrastructure in major cities made them even bigger than was needed at the time they were built, anticipating that more and more people would need water, and they wanted to be sure that the volume of water inside the pipes could push any and every speck of bad stuff coming from homes, schools, hospitals, and industries away from populated areas as fast as possible, even if the population of the city doubled. The waterlines that feed New York City are so big you could drive a semitruck down them.

After the pipes were in the ground, there was no discussion about rerouting them. The waterline was the waterline. You either build so you can tap into it, or go without water altogether. Where water flowed, people were healthy, jobs were created, and cities were born. The population and economic growth of cities like New York, Los Angeles, Las Vegas, Phoenix, Chicago, and Houston hinges on their ability to get water flowing constantly to their populaces.

For decades, the system worked great. But today, a crisis is beginning to appear that was never foreseen by the original designers. The waterworks have never been updated completely, so the pipes underground are decaying, developing holes through which precious water can escape. Our current waterworks system is completely inflexible, and so big that neither changing it, adding to it, or even maintaining it is easy, cheap, or quick. According to the EPA, improvements to existing infrastructure could cost

Figure 8 Water infrastructure has a long history in human society. This image shows the remains of aqueducts used to bring freshwater into Rome during the Roman Empire. Credit: Neil Chambers

$11 billion a year, not to mention what building a whole new infrastructure would cost. Federal agencies along with state and local businesses currently provide less than 30 percent of the funding necessary to maintain clean, drinkable water systems, and as a result water systems across the country are in rapid decline.

♠

The way that water infrastructure functions makes it even harder to conserve water with green buildings. It's true that green solutions, like the WaterSense program described in Chapter 2, can help us reduce the amount of water individual buildings use by as much as a third or more. And a growing number of buildings are implementing conservation and efficiency measures, like gray-water systems and dual-flush toilets. It will not be long before thousands of buildings will have the technologies that save water, and that can translate into smaller water bills from local utilities. But just what would happen if every building in the United States had these technologies? The infrastructure that delivers the water is not equipped to deal with only small volumes of water. Waterworks are based on large volumes in and large volumes out to self-clean and self-sustain themselves. Green building solutions, if implemented by too many buildings, would offset the balance of input and discharge. As it turns out, it is essential for human health to flush lots of water down the drain. If you do not, the volume of water in the sewage system would not be able to move away waste, like excrement, fast enough, which would lead to a myriad of sanitation problems.

Unfortunately, current regulation aimed at conserving water does not take into account what infrastructure needs to function. The EPAct, described in Chapter 2, mandates that water-conserving plumbing fixtures be used in all residential, commercial, and industrial buildings, saving millions of gallons of water each year. But the authors of the bill did not understand that if too little water is flowing into the discharge systems, all that sewage and industrial waste will just sit below cities like Los Angeles or Little Rock. In fact, the EPAct could create a condition where underground sewer systems become breeding grounds for viruses, bacteria, and intestinal parasites. In other words, the very solutions of green buildings to save water could become the cause of people becoming sick with diarrhea, cholera, and typhoid—the very things the original designers of the discharge systems were trying to prevent.

Already, some cities are facing this problem. Not because of green buildings, but because they are shrinking. Such places as Youngstown, Ohio, do not have enough people using the bathroom. Before the steel factories moved to other countries, Youngstown was a fast-growing city of around 200,000 people. After the steel mills left, the city fell into a downward spiral, and people moved out. From 1970 to 2010, more than half of its population left and did not come back. Youngstown, like all other cities, had planned to grow for eternity, and so its infrastructure was designed to deal with more and more people. The waterworks were balanced with large volumes in and large volumes out. When the opposite happened, and suddenly too few people were using the buildings, the sewage systems no longer worked correctly. The result was that the waste just sat in the pipes under Youngstown going nowhere fast. Similarly, if too much water was conserved in other cities like Los Angeles or Little Rock or any other, excrement would not flow out of the discharge system. In the case of Youngstown, they could not dig up the pipes and rebuild, because that would be far too expensive, and much too slow. Something had to be done before people started to get sick, so the city implemented periodic flushes of the sewage systems with freshwater to relieve the problem. They literally had to fill the empty pipes full to clean them out. It is a very wasteful practice, but necessary. They will have to continue to evacuate the water infrastructure with clean water as long as too few people are within the city to balance the system discharge. It illustrates what could happen by reducing water consumption too much with green buildings. We might have, aboveground, strong examples of innovative green buildings full of the latest water-efficient technologies. The architects and developers could proclaim how they are pointing the way to the future. But until we tackle the very serious problem of infrastructure, all the water being saved by low-flow faucets, gray-water systems, water-less urinals, and dual-flush toilets would just be for show.

It is reported that currently 1.2 trillion gallons of sewage, storm water, and industrial waste are dumped into US waters every year. When untreated water escapes into the environment as runoff, or raw sewage, many problems arise. Bacteria can flourish within conditions where waste-water is plentiful. Types such as fecal bacteria are often associated with human health issues. Fecal bacteria are often found in low-lying areas near coastal plains because the topography makes it nearly impossible to not connect storm water with natural bodies of water. These communities try to separate sewer systems from runoff, but water easily finds cracks in the system through which to leak. Bacteria is a common reason for beach closures or lake and river cautions for swimming and sunbathing. When periods of high levels extend for several days or weeks, recreational econo-mies can be harmed if tourism is hampered. Bacteria can deplete oxygen levels within very large bodies.

In the summer of 2004, fishermen off the coast of South Carolina found flounder moving so slowly they could scoop them up without any effort. The flatfish were suffering from hypoxia, a reduction of dissolved oxygen in water that can be harmful to animals. The depletion was so severe that it created a dead zone that was driving suffocating flounder toward the shore. Similar conditions are found throughout the Gulf of Mexico because of wastewater and runoff from Gulf Coast states like Florida, Louisiana, and Texas. When wastewater interacts with ground-water, drinking supplies can be affected. Along with bacteria, a wide spec-trum of chemicals and pathogens are introduced. When this happens, waterborne diseases can affect humans and animals.[8]

Water infrastructure is not just about pipes. Rivers are also irrepara-bly damaged when they are dammed, straightened, and rerouted to move water into human-made infrastructure. Of the 3.5 million miles of riv-ers in the United States, 7 percent are channelized (straightened), while another 17 percent are affected by an estimated 60,000 to 80,000 dams. This comes at a tremendous ecological cost. The US Fish and Wildlife

Service estimates that 70 percent of the land that exists along the banks and slopes of rivers nationwide has been lost or altered. This unique land type is critical for all wildlife, both local species as well as migratory species like songbirds. Freshwater animals are disappearing five times faster than land animals. Over 100 subspecies of salmon and trout are extinct or at risk of extinction within the Pacific Northwest.[9]

An entirely new system needs to be devised to correct the ills of our waterworks system. And the more time we let the problem slide, the more expensive the final solution will become. The current green building industry is not geared toward the fundamental problem of water waste. Already, 40 percent of rivers cannot support aquatic life or be used by humans, while 46 percent of all lakes are in the same condition.[10] Essential ecological features such as wetlands that support vast biodiversity and can reduce flooding and store water for human use are being destroyed by being drained, piped, channelized, and built upon. More than 50 percent of all the wetlands in the United States have been destroyed in the last century. Lake Mead, the major source of water for a huge part of the Southwest, including Phoenix and Los Angeles, is being sucked dry.[11]

Other countries are in even worse shape than we are. Waterways in Asia, for example, contain more lead than any other continent on the planet, posing huge health risks for the populations that depend on them as a water source. In Bangladesh, contamination is widespread. Of the 64 regions throughout the country, the groundwater of 61 has tested positive for high levels of arsenic. The groundwater is accessed by more than 8 million wells across the country, and one in five is now contaminated above the government's drinking water standard. Arsenic is a by-product of the mining and processing of coal.[12] The pollution has been linked to causing one in five deaths within the West Bengal region of Bangladesh, and with millions more exhibiting symptoms such as severe vomiting, disturbances of the blood and circulation, and damage to the nervous system. Long-term exposure to the toxin can cause lung, skin, and bladder cancer. Lack of access to clean water is a large and growing problem. 75 percent of those nations with the greatest percentage of people without access to safe drinking water are in Africa. In 2002, 1.5 million deaths in Africa were attributed to inadequate water supply and unsafe water environments.[13]

These problems can't be fixed with small steps. Big steps are necessary. Reductions in use have to be achieved throughout the water system, as well as measures to rectify the manipulation of rivers, lakes, and streams. Conservation experts suggest 25 to 35 percent of the dams in the United States should be removed. On the negative side, large dams flood lands and displace wildlife and people. Large fish kills are associated with such structures. The natural flows of rivers are permanently altered. In the past, dams have been considered clean power because no carbon emissions are created from energy they generate. This assumption is challenged in a report documenting hydropower dams in forested areas. If vegetation is not removed before the artificial lake forms, the dead material can emit large quantities of methane as it decays. Methane contributes to climate change more than other chemical forms like carbon dioxide or carbon monoxide.[14] The straightening of thousands of rivers has to be rethought. Nature does not work best in straight lines. A more naturally meandering, curving river is best, because it creates a host of niches for different species. It also slows the water, of critical importance for maintaining local climate conditions that species depend on. Finally, rewinding our rivers would dramatically reduce the chance of flooding in our cities and towns. When rivers and wetlands are channelized, the water is drained at an unnatural rate—pushing more water downstream. If this drainage is also associated with areas where forested areas have been removed and runoff amounts are increased, massive flooding will occur. The storm water could be captured for storage for later usage, but with current practices, most, if not all, of the rainwater is lost.

The reconfiguration of water throughout the United States would have long-lasting effects. Correcting the mistakes of the waterworks will not be cheap from the mindset that we can engineer our way out of the problems we have. We have options to make things right, but they fly in the face of existing infrastructure as well as the business-as-usual methods of operation followed by governmental and real estate developers alike.

WATER'S ROLE IN ENERGY PRODUCTION

As stated at the beginning of the chapter, the water used directly in US homes, businesses, schools, and other structures represents only 13 percent of what is consumed.[15] Much more is used to produce services like energy and the materials to create buildings. In the United States, as noted—and also worldwide—most of the water buildings consume is used in thermo-electric power. In this process water is turned into steam to drive gener-ators to make electricity. (This type of energy excludes hydroelectric, or dam-generated, power production.) As the steam turns turbines, the equip-ment can get extremely hot, so large amounts of water are needed to cool it down. All of the heated water is then cooled in cooling towers. As the water evaporates, the temperature drops. Most of the water is released back into the environment. The interdependence of water and energy is why large power-production facilities are located near or at rivers, lakes, and oceans.[16] Climate change could make such a relationship between water and energy stressful. Water levels where some of these production sites are located could dramatically change in the next decade to century. Facilities that are now adjacent to large water bodies could find themselves underwater as lev-els rise, or without access to water because of changes in rainfall or source availability upstream. In terms of cooling, there is no alternative for water. Other methods would be far too expensive. In most cases, power plants do not have to pay utilities to provide the water for cooling because they are taking it directly from a lake or river. In 2000, 195,000 million gallons of water each day were used to produce electricity. If each gallon cost only one cent, that would be an additional $2 billion in cost. Any costs incurred by power companies would be offset to customers. It is important to restate here that most of that electricity is consumed by buildings. The number one way to reduce demand for energy is to reduce energy consumption by buildings. Moreover, the number one way to reduce water consumption is to reduce water used to generate energy and materials for buildings.

So often, pundits talk about the negative effects of fossil fuels and carbon emissions due to power sources. Grand plans are sketched out to change the types of fuels that power our society, and the green buildings of today feature water-saving toilets and faucets. The bigger picture shows that these solutions are a small step. To reduce water consumption we have to rethink the entire water system. Minor improvements in the system are unlikely to bring major returns in terms of saving water or improving quality. The same goes for energy. Buildings have bottomless appetites for energy—and it is infrastructure that is trying to satisfy that desire.

CHAPTER 4

THE ELECTRICAL GRID

As I've explained in the preceding chapters, buildings not only consume more water than any other source but also use more energy than any other source. Most advocates for green buildings cite the studies that say conventional buildings use about 32 percent of all energy and around 68 percent of all electricity generated. But those numbers do not consider the life-cycle costs from building materials or infrastructure. When energy for all the life-cycle phases that contribute to buildings today is added up, including the manufacturing and processing of materials that ultimately go into constructed architecture, buildings are responsible for around 70 percent of all the energy consumed. The result is that millions of tons of coal are burned every year to satisfy buildings' needs. From coal come elevated carbon levels in the atmosphere and particulates that kill more than 13,000 people every year.[1] Consider that if we were able to reduce the amount of energy buildings use by half, the need to find other ways of reducing fossil fuel consumption, such as the use of electric cars, alternative lightbulbs, and renewable energy sources, would be greatly reduced.

Little more than 15 years ago, few people talked about clean energy or solar power. Unlike then, now everyone from global leaders to soccer moms to corporate executives to elementary school students is talking about energy, the issues surrounding it, and its future. As the subject has gained momentum, energy has become a political issue every bit as polarizing as guns, gays, and God. This, in turn, makes it only that much more difficult to get to the bottom of which approaches to energy are truly restorative, destructive, or neutral.

HOW US ENERGY WORKS

Most of the time discussions about energy that are thrown together involve an array of alternatives and strategies, including wind power and turbines, clean coal, natural gas, photovoltaic, solar thermal, utility scale renewable, hydroelectric, nuclear power, tidal, crude oil, wave power, gasoline, electric cars, energy independence, biodiesel, biomass, algae, hydrogen, cleantech, offshore drilling, and geothermal. If that was not confusing enough, often elected officials, experts, and celebrities also talk about sub-sub-parts of the discussion such as building weatherization, energy efficiency, passive solar heating, green jobs and manufacturing, and carbon sequestration. But these are all distractions from the real core problem.

The existing US electrical grid is made up of a vast and complex network of independently owned and operated power plants, pipelines, and transmission lines that transverse the country and then snake into Canada and Mexico. During the last 20 years two things have happened: one, energy demand has increased by 25 percent, and two, funding for improvements has decreased by 30 percent. This includes funding for maintenance of the existing grid. The result is a shortfall of billions of dollars of investment. This has kept the existing system inefficient and unable to keep up with rising consumption. Of the energy generated at any type of power plant, between 6 and 10 percent is lost during transmission. Only about 30 percent of the energy originating from a coal-fired plant is ever used—the rest is lost as heat. Dramatic improvements are desperately needed if the United States is to continue to enjoy a modern lifestyle indefinitely. Of course, the demand for major innovation is stalled for the same reason that retards overhaul of the water system; namely, no one wants to pay for it.

The grid was built when the country had plenty of money and cheap labor. Cheap labor does not exist in the United States anymore. Citizens and officials are weary of spending huge amounts of tax dollars for improvements, so it is much more difficult to make necessary changes. An estimated $550 billion should be invested into the grid each year—that is about the same yearly budget for the Department of Defense. The federal government has not invested that much into infrastructure in 10 to 20 years.

The corporate interests that control the electrical grid are powerful. Large conglomerates own many of the private power plants around the country. They have agreements with local, state, and federal bodies that give them the ability to keep energy costs low for consumers as long as energy consumption remains at a certain level. Utility companies are the middlemen between power plants and consumers, and their revenue models are based on keeping the grid's centralized infrastructure, whereby big power companies control energy generation and profit from usage. Likewise, they create the energy in a small number of huge facilities and then feed it into the grid for eventual delivery to the end user. Centralization of energy production is one of the last "natural" monopolies protected by governments around the world, especially in the United States.

The history behind how we chose such a heavy-handed system stems from a rivalry between Thomas Edison and Nikola Tesla. In 1884, Edison was sure that small localized energy plants were the absolute best way to give people light. This was primarily because he saw direct current (DC) as the most effective medium. Tesla could not have disagreed more. Tesla had immigrated to the United States at the age of 27 to meet his hero, Edison. But unlike Edison, he believed that alternating current (AC) was far superior to DC, and that it could be generated in centralized power plants. The war between the two men would come to be known as the Battle of the Currents. Ultimately, Tesla's vision would win and become the standard for the entire world.

Of the many problems that come with a centralized system, such as loss of energy, cost of infrastructure, and need for maintenance, a much more fundamental problem lies at the center of the discussion, namely the power of the people. In America and most other developed countries (and developing countries), decisions about things like political leaders are made by the people, not by authoritative regimes. The power of the people is likewise seen under capitalism, where the economic strength of a product or service can be greatly influenced by public opinion and purchase patterns. Not so with energy, which is handled as it has always been by a few very powerful and very wealthy individuals, and if you were to decide you wanted to build a microturbine power plant to supply your neighborhood or community with cleaner, cheaper, and more reliable energy, you could get pinched by regulatory agencies with fines adding into the millions of dollars, and maybe even imprisonment. That, at least, is the social cost to the system we have now.[2] Only since 2002 or 2003 have power options like wind, solar, or other sustainable sources been available to consumers, and even today some areas of the country still have no options. People in these regions have to use whatever their utility gives them, and they must pay whatever the utility dictates. Such a stranglehold on a market means that any power created will be bought whether or not it is used by the end user. Coal-fire plants lose 70 percent of the energy they generate, but the consumer picks up the tab for their inefficiency. Transmission lines lose up to another 10 percent, and the end user picks up that tab, too. Advocates for technologies such as smart grids (to be discussed later) say we should improve on the existing system with a list of gadgets and meters. Of course, these gadgets and gizmos will ultimately be paid for by the consumer, not the centralized monopolies that built the grids and keep utility-scale energy production the standard for energy creation in the country.

Surprisingly, the inefficiency of the grid contributes to the profit margins of energy companies. This comes in the form of what energy experts call the baseload demand. The baseload demand is an amount of energy that is assumed will be needed during each hour of the day. It is calculated for each hour, but different times of the day see dramatic jumps in energy consumption. For example, in the morning when people are waking up and starting their day, the normal activities of turning on the morning news to see the weather, alarm clocks going off, and toaster ovens being started all happen around the same time—from 6 A.M. to 9 A.M. Then everyone goes to school and/or work. There, lights are turned on, computers booted up,

Figure 9 Thomas Edison beside original dynamo that led to the electrical grid. Credit: Library of Congress

and heating and cooling systems kick on. This is called a peak load. It is when most of the energy during the day is used. There are two big peak load periods during the day, usually morning and evening. It is the time of day that energy is the most expensive. Every day power companies create enough energy to support the increase of energy being consumed, even if no one ends up using it. If no one uses it, the cost of creating the energy, usually by burning fossil fuels, is still spread among customers. And the pollution from burning the coal still goes into the air.

Say you retrofit your house with as many energy efficiencies as you can. You put in the compact fluorescent lightbulbs, you buy Energy Star appliances, and you weatherize your windows and walls. After the work, you find out that you are using 40 to 50 percent less energy than other homes. You get your power bill the next month, and it is half of what it normally is. For you, it is great. You can see a return on the investment for energy efficiency, but the power company did not stop generating the energy you are no longer using. This is a sobering reality for green buildings in the United States. Over the last 10 years, more than 4,000 green projects have been completed. On average, these buildings are 15 to 20 percent more efficient than standard buildings. The buildings may be using less energy than standard buildings, but the energy generated on their behalf has not decreased.

Moreover, baseload demand is not determined each day but forecast way in advance, in some cases two to five years in advance. To avoid a shortage of energy from a heat wave or cold snap, the utilities produce energy to meet a demand of about 20 to 25 percent above baseload. This ensures that the supply of energy is never affected by unforeseen situations. And though people are replacing incandescent lights with CFLs, the same amount of coal is burned.

THE COMPOSITION OF OUR ENERGY SUPPLY

Energy is used for everything with an on-off switch; energy is always in demand. It is a basic building block for society, and most people would find it impossible to live without it. The United States generates power for the electrical grid in a wide variety of ways, including nuclear, natural gas, wind, hydroelectric, and, of course, coal. Each state's energy mixture is different, based on a wide variety of factors. An energy mix refers to the mixture of electricity within the grid. For example, in New York State the energy mix includes 29 percent of electricity coming from nuclear power, 17 percent from hydroelectric, 16 percent from oil, 14 percent from coal, and about 2 percent from wind, sun, and other renewables. The energy mix in Texas includes 49 percent from natural gas, 37 percent from coal, 10 percent from nuclear, 1 percent from wind, and the rest from an assortment of additional sources. In Colorado, the mix is 70 percent from coal, 24 percent from natural gas, 3 percent from hydroelectric, and 2 percent from wind.[3] Every state is a little different.[4] To really understand the environmental impact of each state, you have to know how much energy is coming from sources that create lots of pollution.

When it comes to electricity, the United States is completely independent. The nation has more coal reserves than any other country. Overall, 80 percent of US energy needs are provided domestically, and there is enough left over that the country exports additional fuel stocks to other nations. Because of the amount of coal that is readily available within the United States, that element will be hard to displace within the energy mix. Globally, the United States uses more energy than any other country. However, China and India are quickly catching up, and will most likely surpass the United States by 2050.

ELECTRIC CARS AND "CLEAN ENERGY"

An ad by the Alliance for Climate Protection (a nonprofit founded by Al Gore in 2006) as part of its Repower America campaign perfectly encapsulates our confusion around energy. In the ad, an older actor dressed in a green hat and flannel button-up shirt (looking something like a straight-talking rugged farmer) walks along a barn with a horse in the background, talking about topics from eliminating dependence on foreign oil to dictators who hate Americans to how current energy is killing "God's green Earth" to the need for green jobs and how citizens need to support clean energy for the good of their children. He uses the term *clean energy* to indicate an appeal for more nuclear power. The ad also focuses on wind and solar power and the need for action now.

The Alliance for Climate Protection did a great job of making high-quality images with short, to-the-point scripts. But the ad did not mention any details that would provide context, and it mixes topics together. It has, unfortunately, become common today for a wide variety of environmental groups and politicians to skew the facts surrounding things like renewable energy and electric cars. As it turns out, the Alliance for Climate

Figure 10 Transmission lines are the standard method for supplying buildings with electricity. Credit: Library of Congress

Protection's perspective on energy generation is not new and unique but very similar to that of oil tycoons and the coal mining industry.

Take, for example, the issue of the people of the United States being addicted to oil. Cars do not use electricity—at least, not yet. A growing number of people, organizations, and more recently automakers have started to push for electric cars. Electric cars are often assumed to offer environmental benefits that would help curb climate change. This is why electric cars are in vogue with media outlets, elected officials, and annual automobile shows.

The theory is that if we replace both the type of engine (from internal combustion engine to electric) and the type of energy (from oil to electricity), we can then tell Big Oil to go stick it while we drive off into the sustainable sunset of tomorrow. This is based largely on the idea that renewable sources will be the major power source for electric cars. The facts say something else. Indeed, the transition from oil-based transport to electric-based transport would have grave ecological and climatic ramifications. By 2030, one in five US vehicles could be an electric or plug-in hybrid model, according to a report issued in November 2010 by Bloomberg New Energy Finance.[5] The Energy Information Agency reports that as more electric cars penetrate the market, they will also drive up electricity demand.[6] Annually, automobiles in the United States use as much energy as those in the United Kingdom use in three years, Iran uses in 3.5 years, Singapore uses in 13 years, and Afghanistan uses in 1,500 years. The increase in electricity demand consequent to the increased acceptance of electric cars will be significant, because the 25 percent of US energy that goes to transportation will stay the same. This is satisfied by petroleum today. If electric cars become the norm, we will see an increase in electricity consumption as more electric cars are sold. This has an awkward effect on the positive outlook of plug-in electrics. If we convert from internal combustion engines to electric cars, the United States would still need that energy to come from some other source. For some states, you may see an increase of renewables to supply some of the new electricity for automobiles, while in others you will see an increase of coal burning to generate the energy needed. Though both petroleum and coal are fossil fuels, gasoline emits fewer carbon emissions than coal. In this scenario, any of the gains accomplished from increased renewable energy projects will have to be directed to automobiles to offset the increased demand for energy. In the scenario pushed by organizations like Alliance for Climate Protection, clean energy can close the gap. When they talk about clean energy, they do not mean wind and solar because they are currently, and for the foreseeable future (say for the next 50 to 100 years), impossible. They think nuclear power is the second best option.

WHY CLEAN ENERGY IS DIRTY

Clean energy is growing in popularity. Whereas renewable energies are created by fuel types that are easily replaced by nature in a short period of time, clean energy is concerned only with carbon emissions. If the amount of carbon emitted during energy production is less than that of a fossil fuel, it is a clean energy. Nuclear power is the best example of this. Even though there is a limited quantity of the primary driver of nuclear power, uranium, and it produces pollution that includes radioactive waste, there are no carbon emissions associated with power generation, so it is officially a clean energy.

But the life-cycle analysis of nuclear energy tells a much different story. From womb to tomb, no other energy source has the potential to negatively affect wildlife, ecology, national security, and human health more than nuclear. In 2006, the British-based magazine *The Ecologist* outlined every step of the process. The article entitled "The Nuclear Dossier" explains that uranium is treated like any other raw material being mined such as iron ore. It is taken from the earth by blasting and digging. The result? Radioactive dust spreads across the landscape into water sources, plants, animals, habitats, fish, and, ultimately, humans. Moreover, the reason nuclear is not considered a renewable resource is because only a very limited supply of uranium is available on our planet.

To enrich uranium, facilities use highly toxic chemicals such as fluorine and chlorine as well as other solvents. It takes about half a ton of fluorine to produce one ton of usable uranium. Fluorine is literally 10,000 times worse for the climate than CO_2. The nuclear industry is not required to keep records of these chemicals' emissions, so there is no way to know how much or how little they affect the atmosphere. The escape of these toxins into the environment should be taken very seriously in considering nuclear as a green option. Enrichment plants in the United States have a nasty track record of leaks. Throughout the decades of the 1980s and 1990s, they released radioactive waste and cancer-causing chemicals directly into the environment. The Paducah Plant in Kentucky was found to have contaminated a nearby aquifer with technetium and carcinogens, prompting a multimillion-dollar cleanup by the federal government. There is nothing truly clean about nuclear except the narrow focus of carbon reduction during energy creation.[7] For every 1,000 megawatts of nuclear power capacity, you get more than 30 tons of high-level radioactive waste per year. The United States has more than 100,000 megawatts of nuclear power installed, so that produces 3,000 tons of waste each year.

This brings to light another problem, which is the storage of radioactive waste. No one wants the garbage created by nuclear plants. Yucca Mountain in Nevada is the resting place for what America creates from electricity consumption. Nuclear waste has to be buried in a way to keep it safe for a million years. Regulatory bodies have stated that storage in facilities such as Yucca Mountain can safeguard radioactive waste for 10,000 years, but that is a mere 0.1 percent of the time necessary to keep the material secure. To put this in perspective, the current evolutionary form humans take (*Homo sapiens*) is little older than a few hundred thousand years. We have no idea where or what the condition of the planet or universe will be in a million years, but clean energy advocates like Alliance for Climate Protection wholeheartedly suggest using nuclear materials as a good and safe energy source for all people and the planet in the name of sustainability. Clean energy is not really concerned about any damage the mining, processing, storing, or installation of the fuel may cause humans or the environment. While it is called clean simply because no carbon emissions are associated with its energy production, it overlooks the harm to humans, water, economies, soil, or ecologies that originates from its creation.

PROBLEMS WITH RENEWABLE ENERGY

What would need to happen for there to be enough electricity for buildings and cars, while not harming the environment? There are good ways to provide the energy for cars that eliminate carbon while at the same time do not cause new problems. Renewable energy is a great alternative to coal and oil—but only when it is in the form of what is called distributed supplies. Distributed energy (also known as the use of micropower plants) is the opposite of the current utility infrastructure of today. It uses small-scale energy sources that decentralize energy production and put the power plants on-site or at least in a noncentralized arrangement. Currently, industrial countries generate most of their electricity in large centralized facilities, such as fossil fuel (coal or gas powered), nuclear, or hydropower plants. These plants have excellent economies of scale but usually transmit electricity long distances and negatively affect the environment. Distributed energy, because it is generated closer to the end user, has less negative environmental impact than do centralized systems. Moreover, smaller units can offset the need for large megawatt power plants which use fossil fuels to produce electricity. In the United States, nearly 84 percent of all electricity comes from fossil fuels—this is partly because we have these enormous power plants procuring energy hundreds of miles away from the end users. Localized power sources would help eliminate the need for fossil fuels. In 2009, renewable energy represented around 8 percent of the total energy consumed.[8] That 8 percent is no small figure—that is enough energy to keep France running for six months, Ireland for ten years, and Afghanistan for almost 400 years. Hydroelectric and biomass make up the majority of renewable energy production. In fact, those two categories represent 85 percent of all the renewable energy created in the United States. Wind and solar make up about 10 percent of the renewable energy created, or between 1 and 3 percent of the overall energy supply for America.[9]

Though solar and wind have a long way to go before they can cover a significant amount of the supply needed for a large percentage of people, the potential is high for both types, and with so much interest in the renewable sector, solar and wind have grown at increased rates during the last decade. By some estimates, solar power could jump to 10 percent of the energy supply by 2025.[10] Solar experts have projected that first the technology will reach about 4.3 percent by 2020, depending on whether or not the industry can attract the estimated $100 billion of investment it would need to grow that fast. The catch to the forecast is that most of the solar power would be generated not by distributed energy but with large utility scale power facilities that would continue to depend on the bulky, inflexible, and expensive infrastructure we currently have. On a global scale, use of solar power has seen increases by as much as 40 percent over the last ten years. In areas of the world that do not have traditional electrical grids, solar power is extremely competitive. In areas that do not incentivize solar energy and that have grid connection, the cost is still too high to be competitive.

Wind power has a very similar outlook. More wind turbines are being installed in the United States than in any other country except China. More than $21 billion of investment has fueled the breakneck speed with which this is happening. According to energy experts at the Lawrence Berkeley National Laboratory, if the pace of new installations stays as it is today, wind power projects could account for 39 percent of all new electric generating capacity added in the United States in the coming years. Wind energy already delivers about 2.5 percent of the nation's electricity supply. Another barrier to expanding the technology for wind generators is the ability to predict whims of weather. Many in the industry say that without substantial improvements in the speed and quality of weather and wind forecasting, the market will be limited. Experts say that computational systems today can't fulfill the task.[11] The space needed for wind farms is substantial as well, and a large-scale infrastructure is mandatory for most conventional plans to scale up wind production in the United States.

While clean energy is focused solely on reducing carbon emissions, some renewable energy sources have a surprisingly hefty ecological and carbon impact. One example is bioenergy, renewable energy derived from living organisms such as plants (most commonly corn), bacteria, or algae. When you compare the emissions from bioenergies, they are less than coal, but they still emit carbon. For example, ethanol, a type of fuel made from corn or sugar, reduces carbon monoxide emissions by 25 to 30 percent as compared to gasoline, but carbon monoxide is still released into the atmosphere when ethanol is burned.[12] Moreover, biofuels like corn, sugarcane, soybeans, switchgrass, wheat, palm oil, hemp, straw, and timber require widespread and intense farming to be highly productive. The fields these cash crops are grown on eliminate the ecosystems previously there. In states like Iowa, where corn and soybean production is high, fields have replaced all but 1 percent of original habitats. Soybeans, sugarcane, and corn take a tremendous amount of energy, water, and management to

Figure 11 Large-scale wind farms can have fragmentation effects similar to highways and other structures, causing negative impacts on ecosystems and species. Credit: US Fish and Wildlife Service

grow, and then even more to process into ethanol, propanol, and biodiesel. In fact, the sustainability of these fuel types is based solely on the fuel at the end of the process. Advocates for products like ethanol do not consider the life-cycle steps that precede its going into a gas tank—this is similar to how most people look at a building as a simple house or skyscraper, thus divorcing it from the pollution upstream.

Today, wind power is generated in 34 states. For wind to replace oil, current production would have to increase by 170 times. In 2008, the US Department of Energy released a report entitled "20% Wind Energy in 2030." The report is a best-case scenario that from 2008 to 2030, if wind doubles every year, it will still represent only a fifth of the electricity needed by the country. The report includes an assumed increase of electricity demand as well, projecting that demand will grow by 39 percent from 2005 to 2030. The increase of electricity demand does not take into consideration a scenario where all cars are no longer using petroleum, having switched to electricity, and how that would explode the need for electricity.

ELECTRIC CARS EQUAL MORE COAL

To create enough electricity from solar and wind power to supply an entirely new fleet of electric cars will take nothing short of a miracle. Conversely, coal is cheap, plentiful, and fast. Facilities already exist, and unlike fuels such as sun and wind, the production is predictable, even schedulable. From places such as West Virginia, where coal is in the mountains, to Montana, where the coal is just underground, the coal industry is set to grow faster and more effectively than any other emerging technology for electricity production. But coal is dirty—it is incredibly dirty—power plants spew all kinds of bad stuff such as mercury, sulfur oxides, selenium, arsenic, and other heavy metals into the environment. Coal production is the largest contributor to human-caused carbon dioxide. The burning of coal causes acid rain. The jobs that are created from coal mining are dangerous and leave the workers with respiratory and other health problems such as lung and other types of cancer. Mining methods such as mountaintop removal used for coal extraction reduce pristine ecologies to wastelands of toxins that cause cancer within people while habitat destruction threatens many species with extinction. Water supplies are impaired, ways of life erased, and people impoverished.

The coal industry along with politicians and advocates talk of how coal can be cleaner and less harmful to the environment. They talk of technologies like clean coal and carbon sequestration techniques. Clean coal technologies are being developed that claim they will have zero environmental impact. Carbon sequestration is a method of capturing carbon, at the time it is either emitted in a coal plant or scooped out of the atmosphere by an additional technology. Once the carbon is ensnared, it is stored in a tank or container. Yet all of these concepts have yet to show any real-world potential. Carbon sequestration is particularly unrealistic.

To store just 10 percent of the carbon emitted in one day would take 41 very large crude carrier (VLCC) supertankers needing nearly 1 billion cubic feet per day. Or, say you wanted to sequester 100 percent of carbon. If you aligned the number of VLCCs needed nose to tail starting at a point on the equator, in less than 280 days you would run into the back of the first one you placed. Currently clean coal is more fantasy than reality.

As noted, if electric cars become widespread, as they likely will, we will have to ramp up coal power plants and nuclear energy to run them. But when you compare the carbon emissions from coal to those from oil, more carbon is emitted from coal, about 20 percent more. As it turns out, oil is a cleaner energy source than coal. Because petroleum has less carbon intensity than coal, it makes no sense to replace it when the result is counter to the goal of climate protection. Electric cars would benefit states such as Colorado and Montana that have large coal reserves to mine, but they are not going to replace fossil fuels or the pollution from them.[13] According to the *Wall Street Journal*, as much as 50 percent of the future electricity needs for electric cars will be met by burning coal. If cars go electric, society would also be more dependent on energy infrastructure, and the problems associated with the grid would be that much worse. In the end we would be adding more coal power plants and nuclear power to the mix to give people enough fuel to drive their kids to school, go on dates, take the family to the mall or park, drive to Grandma's, go to work, and all the other things people do in their cars today. Electric cars are a net negative for human health and the environment.

THE SUSTAINABILITY OF ENERGY

Engineering is a field that people go into when they want to design rocket engines, sewage systems, and air conditioners. Engineering looks at nature and sees inefficiency. Rivers meander over the landscape; this is too slow for civil engineers—so they channelize them and are surprised as floods are higher and cause more damage. So they implement solutions like developing drainage basins complete with ditches, pipes, canals, channels, and culverts to get the water from point A to point B even faster. But this does not help the problems because only more floods come, still worse than the last.

Ecology sees the world from a different set of eyes. The slow-moving conditions of a river are a valuable asset for it. For one, slow has lots of ways to self-correct. Lots of twists and turns distribute high waters across a vast amount of land, as opposed to pointing it in a single direction. When flooding does happen, it is usually into wetland areas where sediment can be dispersed as a way to enrich the soil and thereby improve biodiversity with more nutrition for species to use as food. Dramatic changes are spread across many niches, reducing the amount of impact upheavals have on any specific plant or animal. Imagine a swamp, where a perpetual soup of cloudy water and an assortment of hardy vegetation are present. These conditions are determined by the flatness of the land and the quantity of water pouring into it. The trees and plants along with animals have evolved for the specific patterns within the swamp as it changes throughout the seasons. The shapes, smells, and textures are an indication of what happens throughout the year and a product of wet and drought periods. Other ecosystems like estuaries, riverheads, and creeks are unique based on whether or not the surrounding area is steep, grassy, sandy, or salty as well as the ratio of water to land present. Ecosystems provide a great amount of food and water to lists of species—without energy grids or solar panels. The water systems of river basins to aquifers to streams are cut into the habitats of ancient interactions that enable life to thrive, change, adapt, and flourish. This fact points to clues that exist inside the matrix of ecosystems that indicate a different way of dealing with energy and water—outside the need for massive infrastructure that is too expensive.

Energy production as it exists today is trying to put a round peg in a square hole. The infrastructure and transportation innovations we have attempted have not really solved any problems. The current mentality is that new innovations in technology will fix the problems of the old technologies. As noted, current green building practices are wonderful when trying to reduce utility bills, but they do little to reduce the energy generated upstream. The debate about energy is confusing, sometimes purposefully so and sometimes by accident, and it's been leading us down the wrong path for years. If we continue to try to solve the problems created by using fossil fuels with technology-based sustainability, the only thing we will be making is a mess.

It's time for humankind to look at the problems of energy from a new perspective.

CHAPTER 5

THE SUSTAINABILITY OF NATURE

The term *keystone* comes from architectural history. For ancient architects it was a main element in the development of the arch. First, a number of stones are cut into wedge shapes. Then identical rocks are stacked on opposing columns one on top of the other. Each layer forms more and more of a curve. As the stones meet at a middle point, a keystone is inserted to hold the curvature together. Without it, the arch could not withstand the weight of its own stones and would fall to pieces. With it, the arch could withstand weights 10 to 100 times its weight. The discovery of the arch was critical to the building of structures throughout the ages, including great cathedrals, bridges, and monuments.

A keystone species, also known as an ecological engineer, does the same thing in biological systems. It is a plant or animal that holds an entire ecosystem together by its presence. In the wild, you find a diversity of life unparalleled wherever healthy populations of keystone species exist. The exact species that plays this important role is not limited to higher forms of life like mammals, nor do they always have the same role within nature. For example, some keystone species like African lions and grey wolves are predators. Others such as oysters, kelp, and sea urchins are food sources, and yet others such as oak trees are neither. One thing is for certain: if the keystone species is removed from the habitat, the entire ecology will disintegrate. In oceanic habitats, kelp, oysters, and sea urchins are keystone species because they provide a large array of other animals with food. Kelp and oysters, via

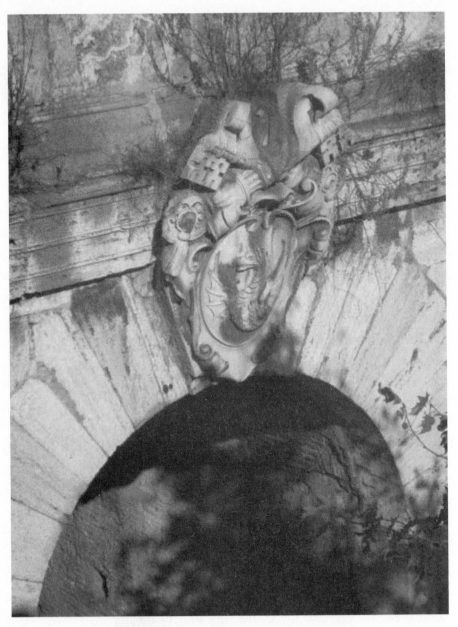

Figure 12 Keystones are a fundamental element in both ancient and contemporary architecture, as this image shows. Second century B.C. keystone in Rome, Italy. Credit: Neil Chambers

the reefs they form, also serve the function of providing shelter for fish, crabs, and other aquatic life-forms. In a tidal marsh, where large populations of oysters can live, the reefs become a microhabitat within the larger tidal marsh/estuarine habitat. Crabs use the reefs to hunt for fish. Adolescent fish use the reefs as hatcheries for their offspring. Active fish and crabs attract birds of prey like herons and egrets that sometimes hunt exclusively on among the oyster beds. Oysters go another step by also being incredible filtering animals. They filter water for food, and in turn remove harmful quantities of bacteria, particulates, and other pollution from the water column. This in turn creates healthier water quality for the entire marshland.

The Greater Yellowstone Ecosystem provides one of the best examples in the United States of the importance of a keystone species to its ecosystem. Spread across Wyoming, Montana, and Idaho and encompassing

Figure 13   The grey wolf is an example of a keystone species. Credit: US Fish and Wildlife Service

20 million acres of land made up of two national parks, six national forests, three national wildlife refuges, Bureau of Land Management holdings, and private and tribal lands, the Greater Yellowstone is one of the largest intact temperate-zone ecosystems on Earth. It is home to hydrothermal features, wildlife, lakes, petrified trees, 67 species of mammals, 322 bird species, 16 fish species, 10 species of reptiles and amphibians, 128 species of butterflies, and more than 1,500 native plants. It has the largest free-roaming herd of bison in the United States and is home to 50 percent of all grizzly bears in the United States and to the rare wolverine and lynx.

At the creation of Yellowstone in 1872, wolf populations were in decline. By 1932, they were all completely gone—exterminated by a combination of hunting and poisoning. Yellowstone has always undertaken innovative efforts to enlarge its boundaries and restore missing links from its biodiversity, and in 1995 grey wolves were reintroduced to the area. Since then researchers have noticed drastic but positive changes.

For years, aspen trees in Yellowstone were thought to naturally grow only in small clumps across the landscape. This growth pattern was seen as natural in Yellowstone. But within five years of wolves being reintroduced, the notion of what is natural for aspen trees changed. The small clusters had transformed into large groves that were fuller and more magnificent than ever before seen. What happened?

For wolves, a major source of food is elk. For elk, a nice meal can come from aspen tree leaves and saplings. For centuries, wolves have known that an ideal hunting area was at the edge of these small collections of aspens. But from the moment wolves were removed from the area, aspen trees were open game for elk. Aspen populations plummeted. When the wolves came back, the elk quickly learned that feeding on them was once again dangerous, so they began to stay away from aspens and grazed more within neighboring wet meadows on grasses and shrubs. Automatically, the aspens began to expand until today, where once only patches existed, groves of aspen covering multiple acres stand strong. The aspen trees are only one example of how wolves can positively affect nature. In Yellowstone, riparian habitats and beaver-pond communities have been restored, songbird populations have recovered, and there is even evidence that grey wolves can buffer the effects of climate change.

Another example of a keystone species in the United States is the grizzly bear. Grizzlies share their status as keystone species with salmon in the Pacific Northwest. Salmon are a prime protein source for a list of species such as other fish, birds, whales, dolphins, seals, and sea lions. They are also rich in nitrogen, sulfur, carbon, and phosphorus. Grizzlies scoop them up during spawning season as they travel upstream to lay their eggs. This is a critical interaction of oceanic nutrients being transferred inland by the grizzlies in the form of fish carcasses and nutrient-rich feces. Because grizzlies hunt in the same spots along a river year after year, studies have been able to show that habitats where the bears typically eat their catch contain higher concentrations of essential minerals that are conducive to other biological life such as trees. Grizzly bears are not just meat eaters. They are omnivores. In fact, they have the eye of a trained botanist for what is edible like berries, roots, grasses, shrubs, and anything else that fits their fancy. They do a lot of digging, and the action turns the soil for new growth of vegetation. All the while they spread seeds of their earlier meals within their scat, which in turn cultivates more areas for their favorite foods.

Keystone species are the cement that holds together ecosystems—or at least they are integral to how an eco-region evolves over a long period of time. Remove them, and problems begin to arise. A negative side effect of such a breakdown is that its ecological services can't be offered. Ecological services are processes that nature does for free—in the case of a forest, it provides everything (including humans) with clean air and water. Wetlands can offer flood protection. Coral reefs and marshland can protect coastal lands from storm surges. These are just a few of the types of services ecologies provide. The prolific quality of these services is directly connected to the number of endemic and native species present along with a lack of toxins and other pollutions. Some keystone species (such as wolves) influence biodiversity by regulating the number of certain kinds of animals while others (such as oysters) attract a host of organisms.

Figure 14   Grizzly bears function as both keystone species and ecological engineers within the wild. Credit: US Fish and Wildlife Service

How a plant or animal becomes a keystone species is tricky to understand. Usually, it is based on the impact of the species as well as the length of time it has persisted within the region. Two things are certain. First, if the keystone species is completely removed from the ecosystem, like the wolves of Yellowstone, biodiversity will collapse and ecological services, like clean water, fresh air, and stable soil, will be impaired. Any other species left in the area, be it frogs, birds, snakes, raccoons, or humans, will suffer. The second certainty is that currently we are not a keystone species.

WHY WE ARE NOT A KEYSTONE SPECIES

Over our comparatively short history, humans have demonstrated a pattern of coming into other species' habitats, setting up camp, and taking over. We like to drink all the water and cut down all the trees. We like to build buildings, roads, ports, farms, and more buildings. Where there are cities and towns and strip malls, biodiversity is greatly diminished.

For example, when the first European settlers found the continental United States, stands of old-growth forests that were thousands of years old stretched for hundreds of thousands of square miles up and down the Atlantic seaboard. There were hundreds of thousands of migratory birds and mammals. There were apex predators like mountain lions and wolves from Maine to Florida to Oregon. There were forests of kelp, mountains of oysters, and millions of beavers. The Great Plains hosted the migration of buffalo, elk, and pronghorn that rivaled the great migrations of other ungulates in Africa. Nearly all of that is gone. We edged them out by over-hunting, overharvesting, overpopulating, or overpolluting their habitat. In their place we built buildings, highways, factories, and farms. We then built water systems and the energy grid to solidify our presence.

Imagine a lone home on the prairie with green grass surrounding. Maybe the house is painted white with dark trim. There could be a 2001 Buick parked in the driveway. Maybe a huge red oak grows in the front yard with an old swing tied to a branch, and a lonely two-lane road runs in front of the house. Not another house is within five miles of this one. You may think, "A house like that could not be doing that much harm." But that house is not the extent of that house. If there is running water in the house, then underground you will find piping that runs from this house of solitude to the next house five miles away, and then to the one after that, and the one after that. They are all connected to a bigger pipe which is connected to a reservoir or an aqueduct. The reservoir is the result of a dam and channelized rivers. The little house on the prairie may be down-stream from the reservoir and is seasonally flooded due to the channelizing of the rivers that make the reservoir that provides the house with water. If the water is ultimately coming from an aquifer, a pump is pulling water from hundreds of feet below the surface. In the Great Plains, the Ogallala Aquifer is the source of most people's water. It is as big as California. All of the farmers in the region depend on it to get their crops to market, which represents more than $20 billion of revenue. Texas has already removed 19 percent of the water from the aquifer, and the water needs in the arid parts of the state are projected to double by 2060.[1] Though vast, the aquifer is not infinite. Since the 1930s the water level in the aquifer has dropped over 100 feet.[2] In 2009 alone, the water in the aquifer dropped about 1.5 feet. In places where corn production is especially intense, average annual declines have been found that exceed eight feet. The rate of withdrawal is faster than rainfall can replenish the aquifer, and between 50 and 60 percent of the underground great lake could be gone by 2060.[3]

If there are lights on in the lone house on the prairie, it is connected to the grid, and there is a good chance a large percentage of the electricity used is from coal or nuclear. This isolated house is a heavier user of energy than other houses because it is so far away from everything else that power plants have to create extra energy to compensate for what is lost through transmission lines. This translates into the creation of even more pollution and higher carbon emissions to serve this single house. You have to add the life cycle to the image of that nice little house in the middle of nowhere to get the real picture.

The full picture is that we are not a keystone species. If a keystone species is an organism that holds an ecosystem together, then we are the opposite of that. The best description for us would actually be an anti-keystone species. The way we have developed our society is so disruptive that even if you figure out how to use all green nontoxic materials for the construction of your house or skyscraper and avoid potentially making yourself, your coworkers, or your family sick, you are still highly likely to be exposed to contamination from things like arsenic and mercury that are pumped into the environment from other sources. These contaminants come from all the other building materials you may not have bought but that others did use for their projects. Moreover, what are the materials you are using? Often manufacturers will call their products green for one small feature. A great example is bamboo. Between 2005 and 2008, bamboo anything was the big craze—bamboo flooring, cabinets, tables, shelves, and even clothing. Not all bamboo is created equal. Some of it is farmed with deadly pesticides and replaces valid ecosystems. I have found bamboo flooring in major home improvement stores that is called green but still contains VOCs and other toxic chemicals. Bamboo is a choice product, meaning you can choose to use it or not. For larger projects like high-rises, hospitals, malls, highways, and sidewalks, you have to use concrete and steel. There are ways to reduce these projects' impacts, but you can't erase them. Less poison is still poison.

KEYSTONE ENGINEERS

Take beavers. They are builders just like us. You can't teach a beaver how not to cut down trees and start damming up a stream. They are built to build. If you took 100 beavers and let them loose in a forest of creeks, streams, and trees, they would start building a dam within days, and they would not stop until they were finished. They would do it anywhere they could. Like humans, they like to move in, take over, and start cutting down trees. They are highly intelligent when it comes to engineering a dam. A group of researchers poked small holes in different beaver dams to see what the beavers would do. Every time, the creature would realize something was going wrong because of the drop in water level, search out the hole, and patch it. No matter the location of the hole, the beavers would find it. The result of such wonderful dam building is that a small creek becomes a big pond fast. The water backs up and floods the forest behind it. Likewise, to build such a great structure, the semi-aquatic rodent needs lots of sticks, twigs, and trunks. The animal actually eats through the hard fleshy part of the tree to cut it down. Any damage caused to its teeth due to pigging out on bark vanishes in a matter of two to three days because its teeth continuously grow. Its four incisors are made of hard orange enamel on the front and a softer dentin on the back. The chisel-like ends of the incisors are maintained by their self-sharpening wear pattern. The beaver is a tree-eating machine.

A beaver will usually not start building anything until it finds a mate. Beavers mate for life, and only after two beavers find each other does the building begin. It is not just dams that beavers build well; they also build canals and housing with great skill. As the dam gets bigger and more water is held behind it, they need more and more wood. After a few weeks, all the easy-to-get wood has been used; typically these are trees about four to eight inches wide. The only things that are left are big fat trees. A beaver is not big enough to carry such a large log—but that is the beauty of how they build canals. Water displaces the weight. They dig canals to the foot of bigger trees, chew them down, and then float them to where they want them. It is pretty easy once the tree is in the water. Beaver lodges are not just homes but fortresses. The only entrance to a lodge is underwater, and the top is made of mud, sticks, leaves, and anything else beavers can find. To break through it would take a jackhammer, something most predators do not have handy.[4]

Beavers are very much like us. They are incredibly intelligent, as expressed by their ability to solve unique problems. And just like us, their building behaviors and the rate at which they use materials is unsustainable. Over a few seasons, they have exhausted the natural resources they need—namely trees. They cut so many down that none are close enough even to reach by canal, so they abandon their homes for lands with more plentiful wood.

The natural behavior of beavers has a tremendous influence on the ecosystem. Large areas are clear-cut and then flooded by their daily routine. Like beavers, we also have a tremendous influence on ecosystems. A great example is the Hoover Dam. The dam provides several services to the Southwest, namely by generating electricity, providing flood protection, and making water available for agriculture and people. In many ways, the Hoover Dam sets up the opportunity for environmental impacts such as overpopulation in arid states like Arizona and Nevada. The crowded cities of Phoenix and Las Vegas are having to spend billions of dollars to deal with how water supply is not meeting demand. This and other impacts on the environment from the dam are beginning to outweigh the positives.

The first apparent effect is on the natural flow of the Colorado River. Damming it, the engineers created a severe influence on the habitats and communities both upstream and downstream. Because Hoover is so huge, the magnitude of the consequences is dramatic. A subtle but important direct effect is the temperature of the water on either side of the structure. Before the construction, the temperature of the waters changed during different seasons. But after the dam was completed, its turbines lowered the water temperature, resulting in the extinction of several fish species. The chemistry of the water is different today as well. Water exiting Lake Mead, created by the dam, has higher concentrations of dissolved salts and lower oxygen levels than would be the case for a free-flowing river.[5] The lake loses 350 billion gallons of water every year to evaporation because it is in a desert area that is extremely hot and dry.[6] Sediment builds up behind the dam, allowing clear water to flow out. The Colorado River carries little sediment as it flows from the dam, and this has an erosive effect on the river channel and banks. And the lack of sediment eliminates shorelines and reduces the nutrients entering biologically productive coastal regions such as estuaries and marshlands.

Dams also affect keystone species. First they block the migration of salmon upstream to their spawning streams. Scientists have created fish ladders as well as management schemes that transport the fish around the obstacles, but these efforts have limited success. As salmon are separated from the ecological functions of a habitat, other keystone species are impacted. In this example, it would be the grizzly bear. Without a large amount of salmon, grizzly bears cannot transport the amount of oceanic nutrients inland to help enrich soils for trees. Lack of vegetation cover then affects songbirds and small mammals. If these species disappear, the animals that hunt them disappear. Rivers that do not produce a bonanza of salmon will not attract bears. They migrate to other areas entirely, creating a gap at the center of the ecological arch.

The Hoover Dam stands 726 feet high and is 45 feet thick at the top and 660 feet thick at the bottom. That makes it larger than the Great Pyramid of Cheops (which is the oldest and largest of the three pyramids in the Giza Necropolis). It is almost entirely made of concrete, nearly 3.25 million cubic yards—so much, in fact, that you could pave a road 16 feet wide and 8 inches thick from San Francisco to New York City with the amount used to build the dam.[7] The structure is so massive that if people just walked away from the dam today, and no one maintained it, fixed it, or repaired it, the dam would stand as it is for the better part of 5,000 years before it would actually breach.

This highlights another prime point for keystone species. Whereas we build things to last, the influence of key species is always temporary. The thing about beavers' dams is that as they are built, the pond they create provides hunting grounds for birds and mammals. They also provide spawning grounds for salamanders and frogs. Once the dam falls apart and the area has had all the trees removed, a bloom of new growth happens. Saplings, wildflowers, and grasses sprout up. Fields with lots of sunlight will first see fast-growing trees like fur and pine. In the gaps, slower-growing trees like oaks and cherry will grow. The forest is replenished with thin and fat trees. Over time, the stream returns to pre-beaver conditions. And that is just about the time a new beaver pair move into the area to start the process all over again. The process of beavers coming into areas, cutting all the trees down, building a dam, and then moving out has been going on for millions of years. The behavior encourages not just one type of tree but lots of kinds of trees, and a host of other unique niches without which hundreds of other species couldn't survive. Beavers and the forests have become mates for life.

The other thing to learn from beavers is that they are unsustainable only within a small area of the forest. They build only at streams and creeks, so there are only a few places they can build. This localizes the damage to the forest. If they could build anywhere, they would cut the forest down like a lawnmower. This would not be very helpful in creating niches for other species. So, it is OK to be unsustainable as long as it is in small spots. For example, you can build a strip mall along a river, and that would not cause much damage. But you can't build a strip mall, an interstate highway, and 40,000 houses that line the entire length of the river. That is too much damage.

These two lessons learned from the beaver underline the biggest problem buildings cause to the environment. The troubles caused by energy and water usage, the pollution that is spewed into rivers and the air by manufacturing, and the damage caused by infrastructure are nothing compared to how we continue to spread out across the landscape, never allowing the ecosystem that was once there to recover. We don't just take up an area around a creek or a river or even an ocean. We take it all, and we give none of it back. To us, it was ours in the first place.

THE FINAL COMPONENT OF WHAT A BUILDING IS

This is the final component to what a building is: Buildings are eaters of land. I have talked about the damage done to the environment and the atmosphere by modern building practices, but these would be less of a problem if the actual building of yards, houses, roads, and utility scale renewable energy did not displace every other living thing.

For green buildings to make real change they must focus more on the bigger picture of what buildings are, and focus less on the more conventional idea that a house is a house. Green building has its heart in the right place. Its goal, presently, is to help people find solutions for problems like toxic materials and inefficient energy usage that they can implement easily and quickly. Green building also wants to reduce the environmental impact of how we live on the planet by finding more sustainable energy sources and not polluting the water supply and the atmosphere. But it has no solution for the real problem of humankind's quick and efficient displacement of nature. Green building today is using a little more compassion but still kicking nature's butt.

In June of 2006, I was on the phone with Dr. Viviana Ruiz, then an ornithological doctoral student at Cornell University. She specializes in how birds interact with urban areas in both developed and developing countries. At the time, she was quite busy with her thesis research, yet I had convinced her to take a "mere five minutes" out of her workday to help me grasp the phenomenon of why there are 275 species of birds found in Manhattan's Central Park. I was working on a nearby project that I was hoping could restore a diverse bird habitat but was worried it would attract only Canada geese. I wanted to create something that was as diverse as Central Park. Ruiz explained to me that lots of birds go to

Central Park because most of the area surrounding it is covered over with buildings, roads, and the like. The other reason so many birds show up in the park is that there are lots of variations of predators and prey. There are squirrels for peregrine falcons and redtail hawks. There are fish for herons and egrets, ponds for ducks and swans, trees for woodpeckers and robins, and low-lying shrubs for wild turkeys. My five minutes had turned into an hour and a half, and our talk had drifted from Central Park to her passion for fowl populations in Costa Rica. She was explaining to me that bird species were disappearing from the national forests of the Latin American country in remote areas. I could hear the anxiety in her voice to get back to her studies, but I was engrossed. Like a little schoolboy, I was peppering her with questions every time she paused to catch her breath. As she was explaining that, generally, populations of birds were dropping because habitat was disappearing at the outskirts of the national forests, I said something like, "Yes, right, land is disappearing," and as I started to form another question, Ruiz cut me off and said bluntly, "No, the land isn't disappearing! The land is still there! It's the stuff on the land that's disappearing. And do you know what's replacing it?"

"Uh…" Suddenly I had nothing to say.

Annoyed, she continued, "Buildings!"

Buildings? Just plain old buildings are the biggest problem. Costa Rica does not have the same dependence on fossil fuels as the United States, nor does it have the same level of infrastructure. The country generates nearly 90 percent of its electricity from renewable sources such as hydroelectric. The pollution associated from coal is not an issue. Water use is limited and sustainable. In fact, Costa Rica is an ideal green world. The factors that we normally associate with adverse effects on species and ecological health are not present. The country recognizes the value of its connected habitats, and it has tried to minimize the extent of human development. Yet the patterns and sizes of development in the country are still too big, and are too disruptive within ecosystems. Plus, the buildings that are in the forests, and that make up the cities, are permanent, thus solidifying disruption for long periods of time. This all adds up to be enough to cause the disappearance of species.

There's more bad news for Ruiz's passion—of the 10,000 species of birds worldwide more than 1 percent have already disappeared in the last half century. Presently, another 12 percent are severely endangered with a high probability of half of them being lost within the next 100 years. Jan Schipper, of the International Union for Conservation of Nature, spent five years with almost 2,000 scientific colleagues surveying the state of mammals on the planet. Of the 5,487 known mammal species, 52 percent of them are declining and one in four is facing imminent extinction. In some cases, such as that of the Baiji dolphin, a freshwater dolphin found only in the Yangtze River in China, the species is functionally extinct— meaning that there are not enough living to avoid what scientists call inbreeding depression and genetic drift, and if there are living specimens, they are the last to ever exist. E. O. Wilson, the renowned biologist, esti- mates that 30 to 50 percent of all species in the world will be wiped out by 2050 if trends toward habitat destruction and human development con- tinue.[8] Humankind has managed to identify 1.5 million species, but that is a mere fraction of the tens of millions that may be present in nature. Of course, this could mean that some species will disappear before we even know they exist.

Today, the current rate of extinction is a thousand times greater than the average rate of extinction over the earth's history. The way we build is causing a massive extermination of living organisms comparable only to the K-T extinction event that wiped out the dinosaurs 65 million years ago.

For all the good green buildings do for the environment, the one thing they do not do is deal with the problem of how their physical existence affects nature. As outlined in Chapter 2, current practices within green building are focused on the five areas of reducing the amount of energy buildings consume, changing the types of energy buildings use, improv- ing the types of materials used for construction, eliminating practices that waste water, and mitigating problems with indoor air quality. None of these really address the problem of how buildings, and the infrastructure necessary to support them, take up so much space. Nor do any of the five areas address the permanence of buildings. While architects, engineers, and designers labor to reduce the carbon or ecological impact of a building, its physical impact is causing mayhem throughout the natural world.

Take Dr. Ruiz's favorite subject of birds, for example. Over a billion birds are killed every year by colliding with buildings. Probably three times that number are injured. Birds collide with buildings because they perceive glass as open air, and so they think they can fly right through it. Many modern buildings, including skyscrapers, are made with large pieces of glass that reflect trees or the sky. Birds do not know the reflection is not a tree until it is too late. Techniques to prevent birds from slamming into a building have been around for years. Simple things like using ultraviolet tape on windows can reduce collisions because birds can see ultraviolet tape, even though humans can't. Architects can slope windows just slightly so they do not reflect trees and the sky. But none of these methods are popular. Architects love big pieces of glass. One told me that it was because glass allows you to feel inside and outside at the same time. I wondered, why don't you just go outside? Bird-friendly measures have been taken for other things—you can buy bird-friendly coffee for instance—but the biggest killer of birds has yet to catch our attention.

The effects of glass on birds are just the beginning of how buildings and human development affect nature. We build things that cover over wetlands, woodlands, forests, and grasslands that constitute precious mating grounds and hunting areas. Natural corridors, which act like interstate highways for wildlife to move across the landscape, are blocked, disrupted, and completely destroyed. Highways have become immovable blockades cutting off water supply to countless animals. If you have ever done a fair amount of driving, you are very familiar with the frequency with which animals are killed by cars. Highways are implacable structures of concrete and steel, four to ten lanes wide, with cars speeding in different directions. Because a highway's profile is thin and very long, it gives animals no choice but to try to cross. In standard construction, roadways are laid directly on the ground and can cut a fragile habitat into two chunks. Sometimes, these structures cross directly over natural corridors that have been used by species for thousands of years.

Conservationists refer to the slicing of natural areas into pieces by highways and other development as habitat fragmentation. The fragmentation knocks the habitat out of balance. Just as a dam stops the transfer of salmon nutrient from reaching the forest floor, fragmentation disrupts the normal interaction of species. Take the case of the red wolf, an important keystone species that had been decimated in places like North Carolina. Without the *Canis lupus* present, prey-to-predator equilibrium was nonexistent. This caused an explosion of whitetail deer.[9] The populations of deer were also expanded by the diverse wooded areas of the Southeast being transformed into lawns as subdivisions replaced forests. In the 1930s, prior to the removal of the red wolf, estimated whitetail populations were as few as 300,000. Current populations range in the tens of millions. Overpopulation has been the reason for many deer deaths due to malnutrition during the winter.[10] Too many individuals also cause massive sickness throughout a much wider range of a population. In 2002, the Southeastern Cooperative Wildlife Disease Study found that specimens from Georgia to Pennsylvania and as far west as Texas, Kansas, and Wisconsin had been infected by two diseases: epizootic hemorrhagic disease and bluetongue.[11]

Reintroduction programs for the red wolf that started in 1987 in the Alligator River National Wildlife Refuge, in northeastern North Carolina, promised to rebalance deer populations. Since then, the area has grown to include three national wildlife refuges, a Department of Defense bombing range, state-owned lands, and private property spanning a total of 1.5 million acres. Over 100 red wolves roam their native habitats in five northeastern North Carolina counties, and approximately 200 comprise the Species Survival Plan captive breeding program in sites across the United States, still an essential element of red wolf recovery.[12] The reappearance of the wolves has rebalanced the number of deer in the release areas to a more natural state.

Fragmentation is a serious problem for red wolves and other species. As subdivisions, infrastructure, cities, and other built objects are scattered across the landscape without consideration of how the lands they occupy affect biological and ecological systems, populations are separated into remote places that can't maintain a healthy gene pool, thereby setting off the dynamic of extinction without one animal ever being killed by a human. In the case of the red wolves, this occurred in the form of wolves mating with coyotes, a nonnative species of North Carolina. In other circumstances, birth defects such as hip bone deformity arose in populations, making it impossible for affected wolves to hunt successfully or to give birth.

What was once fertile ecology is now concrete, asphalt, steel, and other assorted building materials. Contemporary society usually thinks species are endangered because their current habitats are being destroyed, but the truth is that many species live in the small fragmented habitats we identify as theirs only because we are using every other place they would usually live. How we create buildings, produce energy, conceive of infrastructure, and use energy is counter to how ecology works and thrives. So we can't just make small adjustments to the things we create, conceive, produce, and use. Rather, we need to totally reinvent the process. This is not to say that green buildings aren't good, or that aspects such as energy efficiency and water conservation aren't useful, but architecture as a whole is still practiced by guidelines and rules that make us the antithesis of a keystone species. And even a deep commitment to green building can't make it more ecological simply by piling better insulation or gray-water systems onto the problem. We must reenvision the role of green architecture and embolden it to go beyond anecdotal solutions to find bigger and more amazing solutions for living in harmony with nature.

In the following chapters, I will show what designers, architects, and engineers can learn from the growing field of urban ecology. Situated at the intersection of wild places and human development, urban ecology looks at how species interact with urbanized areas such as suburbs and cities. It is unique in that it does not see humans, or the things we build, as separate from nature.

Urban ecology is also involved with the concept of ecomimicry. The goal of ecomimicry is to be a proxy for ecology. In cities, the natural ecological function such as water purification or moisture retention has been offset by streets, buildings, and human populations. This creates a gap between the human world and the natural world—and promotes the ill-advised concept that people are not part of nature. Ecomimicry considers wilderness and urbanization as one thing, so it reimagines how both can be beneficial to each other.

Recall two very powerful hurricanes of the last quarter century, Andrew and Katrina. Two of the strongest storms to make landfall during the last hundred years, they both caused devastating damages. The difference was in how damaging the storm surges were in each area. In Florida, marsh and wetlands had been restored to some degree before Andrew hit in 1992. Some flooding occurred, but not to the extent of New Orleans with Katrina in 2005. The wetlands and swamps on the southern tip of Louisiana are heavily impaired. Imagine rethinking architecture, and green buildings, to the point that buildings are designed not according to styles or materials but to reignite the ecological benefits of nature.

We could have a similar positive influence on biodiversity—just like wolves or beavers. The goal of ecomimicry is to take entire cities (such as New York City or Paris or New Delhi) and redesign them in ways that "reenact" the functions of ecosystems. Projects are ongoing in the Chesapeake Bay, as well as in a small estuary called Withers Swash in South Carolina, that are bridging the gap between buildings and nature. They are using oysters to improve health conditions as they also reestablish ecosystems. Green building is currently much more interested in nontoxic paints and energy options. However, other designers and scientists are at the forefront of a new truly green era—one where we move into a keystone role on this planet. Such a move could mean we will see the end of architecture as we know it.

CHAPTER 6

THE CITIES OF TOMORROW

Between the years 2010 and 2020, green building projects are projected to go from approximately 4,000 completed to around 30,000 completed projects, but that is a fairly small number compared to the number of new buildings completed each year, as well as the number of buildings that exist. For green buildings to decrease our water and energy usage (overlooking the need for infrastructure overhauls) by the year 2060, I would venture to say that more than 75 percent of all homes and commercial buildings would need to be green. Moreover, homes across the United States would need to be at least 20 to 30 percent more energy efficient than they currently are, and water consumption would need to drop by 40 to 50 percent.

That is not what is being forecasted. As stated above, only about 30,000 buildings will be green—and that is combining homes and commercial projects. So what will that mean if it happens? Will it do much good? Green buildings today, as defined by the LEED Rating System, are only required to meet, and then begin to exceed, national standards for energy consumption. In the green profession today, 14 percent is viewed as a success; however, if 30,000 buildings are on average 14 percent more energy efficient, you would not see a change in power generation within the country. In fact, if only that many buildings are green by 2020, overall electricity production will increase, not decrease. Why? Because that is not enough to offset new energy consumption coming from an increase of new buildings. On average, between 500,000 and 800,000 new commercial buildings come online every year, and add to that millions of single-family homes that are built each year. In addition to new buildings, there are still the millions and millions of existing buildings such as offices, retail operations, hospitals, houses, and grocery stores. As new projects come online, they will also need more energy from the grid. Alternative sources, like wind and solar, are not growing fast enough to meet the growing demand. This will mean more coal and other fossil fuels. The savings will be eclipsed by the need before the savings can be realized. If the goal is to have all buildings around the world save energy in accordance with LEED guidelines—say, the 14 percent it mandates—the overall savings is even less. A mere 3 percent reduction would be realized on a global scale. This is no success at all. When I have pointed this out to other experts within the green industry, they typically say that such numbers may be small, but they are a start. I would caution anyone from believing that this is a start. It has taken the LEED movement more than ten years to get to the point where it could become the building standard, and changing it again would take just as long, in which period more buildings would be built and more energy would be needed. If we continue on our current course, we are on track to make the environment worse in the future than it is today. The goal of 30,000 green buildings is far too small, and current standards for green buildings are not bold enough to foster the necessary change for us to reduce our dependence on toxic fuel sources, expensive infrastructure, or dirty building materials. As noted earlier in the text, if there is one shortfall with the green building movement, it is that the majority of green technologies are focused on individual structures. This overlooks the role of cities, and it overshadows the effect that retrofitting larger systems could have on improving ecological services.

CITIES

Nearly everyone in the developed world lives in or near a city. Cities are the economic engines of their surrounding communities, providing a majority of financial growth such as jobs, services, income, revenue, and property values. Cities used to be small. At the turn of the twentieth century, only about 10 percent of the world population lived in urbanized areas. The trend toward urbanization moved very fast in the early part of the century. In 1900, only about 40 percent of the American population lived in urban areas; today that percentage has doubled. In the 1960s and 1970s people started moving just outside of core cities. The transition from the traditional living situation within a city into suburbs gave them the ability to live where they could own a home and have a backyard for their kids while they could still go to work in the city and enjoy the culture it provided. Most people think of an urban area as a city such as Los Angeles or Houston, but that is a concept largely replaced by what an urban area is today.

If you land at the airport in White Plains, New York—about 45 minutes outside of the city limits of New York City itself—you would still be under the influence of the city's economic engine. This larger entity that encompasses New York is called a metropolitan area. Though you may still think of New York as Wall Street or Midtown, those are out-of-date concepts. In the past, the economics of a city were solidly situated in the core city, but today core cities like New York, Chicago, and all other major cities are more dependent on their surrounding areas than on their own citizens. Metropolitan areas, or simply metros, are the dominant figures within the landscape of suburbs and cities. It is the physical boundary the financial influence has on a region. The metro area as a whole determines the population and how crowded it is. As more people move into the outskirts of a core city, two things happen. If it is a fairly undeveloped area, new roads, waterworks, and energy production are needed. If it is a previously developed area, upgrades of basic infrastructure are necessary. From the perspective of ecological services, both activities fragment the land even more—or in the case of predeveloped areas, the new construction flushes out any last standing remnants of nature that may have survived.

A metro area is usually much larger than the core city—sometimes by a factor of five to six times—and will have an overall population much bigger. However, the density of people (that is, the number of people per square mile) will be far lower in a metro area than in a core city. For example, the NYC metro area has a population between 19 and 21 million people, while the core city of New York has a mere 8 million. Such places as Putnam Valley, New York (population: 11,000), or Palmyra, Pennsylvania (population: 3,145), are both more than an hour away from New York, the core city of the metro area they belong to.

Metro areas are so dominant that the top twenty metros, which in addition to New York include the cities and surroundings of Chicago, Detroit, San Francisco, and Atlanta, comprise more than 40 percent of the population of the United States. And though they seem to sprawl all over the landscape, they are fairly compact compared to how populations of people once dwelled on the land. For example, a traditional farming community takes up eight times more space than a city or suburb. In major cities, density can reach between 10,000 and 28,000 people per square mile. In smaller cities and towns, the number drops to 600 to 5,000 people per square mile. Rural areas can have anywhere from 3 to 66 people per square mile.

MEGACITIES

A city can be any size, so long as it is the core economic engine of the surrounding area. When a city is home to between 250,000 and 4 million people, it is considered a major city. Megacities are core cities that house 5 million people or more. The thing about megacities is that they are so big and have such an influence on the region that their metro area starts to run into other metropolitan areas. New York is a megacity, but directly to the north and south of New York are other major cities. About four hours north is Boston, and a little more than two hours south are Baltimore and Washington, DC. Each of these cities has its own metropolitan area. Boston metro includes much of the eastern part of Massachusetts, while the Washington and Baltimore metro areas overlap one another to encompass parts of Virginia and most of Maryland. The combination of the four metro areas forms a megalopolis that blurs the lines of traditional boundaries like state and city limits.

MEGALOPOLISES

A megalopolis (also known as a mega-region) is a collection of cities and megacities that bolster the economic potential and growth of one another to the point that it becomes more and more difficult to tell where one city's economic engine starts and stops. In the Boston–New York–Baltimore–DC megalopolis, essentially what is happening is that the entire region from Boston to Washington, and even farther south to Richmond, Virginia, has become one megalopolis, propelling financial growth and reinforcing itself as a single economic organism. The formation of a megalopolis comes when metropolitan areas begin to overlap. It is not unheard of for people to commute to a city from two or two and a half hours away. In the case of New York, this is very common. However, two hours north of the city you begin to run into the metropolitan area of Boston. You may actually work in New York and pay taxes in Massachusetts. You could easily find a job in White Plains, New York, that would make your commute 45 minutes shorter. If you have children, you may send them into Boston or its surrounding areas for their education. Doing so makes you interconnected with the financial engine of Beantown.

This type of scenario is happening throughout the Boston–New York–Baltimore–DC megalopolis, where people live in one metropolitan area, work in an adjacent one, and are connected to a third. This is how these corridors function as a single entity, and they can no longer be defined by the boundaries of core cities, individual states, or metropolitan areas. Megalopolises are the conglomeration of all these different metro areas, cities, and all the little towns, suburbs, and urban areas in between. They blur the boundaries of where one place starts and the other stops, forming a new geographic entity. They are interlocked by economic systems, shared natural resources and ecosystems, and transportation systems that connect city to city and suburb to suburb.[1] They are the driving force for where people live, work, and travel. No one point, such as a core city, can be identified as the sole producer of culture or prosperity.

There are an estimated 40 megalopolises around the world. North America has a total of 13. Europe and Asia have 12 each, South America has two, and the Middle East has one. Of those in North America, ten are completely within the boundaries of the United States, two are a combination of US and Canadian zones, and one is made up of Mexico City and surrounding areas. Some have strange names like NewHousRougeacola and LosLongDiegoVegas, which describe the megalopolises of the Houston–New Orleans–Pensacola area and the Los Angeles–Long Beach–San Diego–Las Vegas area, respectively. Others have tamer titles such as Cascadia, which defines the Seattle–Portland–Vancouver megalopolis. It is important to note that these areas are dynamically interconnected by bulging populations in the millions, economic centers that interact daily, and people who move throughout them often. Culturally, they can be very different or share similar common goals and histories.

HOW THE MEGALOPOLIS WILL CHANGE GREEN BUILDING TOMORROW

Nearly 100 percent of all future construction of green buildings, and buildings in general, will happen within a megalopolis. Practically every American is living in a megalopolis currently, or will be within the next 10 to 20 years. And in some ways, these megalopolises are a blessing in disguise. By concentrating people into a smaller land area, they can efficiently produce employment for millions and millions of people. If you live in a small town between New York and Baltimore, your opportunities during a job search are greatly improved.

The compact nature of megalopolises also allows civilization to move toward a more harmonious relationship with nature. If more people are living in dense areas, the opportunity for solutions like mass transit and highways is greatly improved. However, megalopolises can also be a disaster waiting to happen. The concentration means the need for massive amounts of new infrastructure to support the population. Megalopolises will have to look far beyond their borders to find enough water and energy to feed the never-ending need for lighting, sewage disposal, and other necessities for their citizens, potentially further degrading the natural land surrounding them. This is why dealing with individual buildings is not enough for green building.

The next half century will see a growth in infrastructure such as waterworks and the energy grid such as has never been seen before if we are going to try to keep pace with the population growth projected in cities and urban areas around the world. Globally, 50 percent of people today live in cities. By 2050, 75 percent of people will live in urban areas. Already 80 percent of Americans live in an urbanized location. Most jobs are available in urban areas—and suburban areas are seeing the fastest growth of employment compared to core cities. It is reasonable to assume that the next few decades will see the trend of people moving into mega-regions continue, thereby strengthening the trend more. Rural lifestyles are being abandoned in the Great Plains region.[2] The economic engines of farming and ranching can't support new large populations. As people move away, they go to where jobs are, which is typically in preestablished metropolitan areas.[3] In the case of the Great Plains, so many people have left that most of the half million square miles in the middle of the country stretching from Alberta, Canada, to the deserts of western Texas are practically empty.[4]

The trend toward megalopolises is global—and it is transforming how basic components of society work. In the early years of the twentieth century, the city was the place for all activities of life—from manufacturing jobs to office jobs. The shift to globalized economics means that the core city is no longer the location of all events, but also that its reach is far broader. A company might have offices in New York while its manufacturing is done in the Chinese countryside. Though the company's operations are in two different countries, they are part of the same economic engine.

Megalopolises present a serious challenge for infrastructure. Cities, megacities, and megalopolises are applying unprecedented pressures on natural resources. In 2003, the Northeast and Midwest of the United

States along with Ontario, Canada, experienced what it means when things break down within megalopolises. The Northeast Blackout of 2003 caused a widespread power outage that affected 55 million people. The blackout lasted only two days in most areas, and only a few fatalities were reported. The event did highlight that existing policies were not designed to mandate reliable supplies of energy from the infrastructure —nor were safeguards in place to eliminate the possibility of such a system failure. A binational task force concluded that overgrown trees in Ohio had caused the initial problem that began a cascading shutdown of more than 100 power stations, which reduced energy output by 80 percent.

Fortunately, the breakdown of the grid occurred during a relatively mild August, but the blackout could have caused many more fatalities if it had occurred during an extreme heat wave. That is exactly what happened in Europe during the same year.

Environmental problems can spiral out of control when the dynamic of megalopolises are international as well as local. Heat waves are likely to increase in the future. Increased hot periods will also lead to an increase in droughts. If dry seasons become the norm too, it will put many megalopolises in a dire situation. If shortages of water occurred at the scale of the Northeast Blackout for any length of time, the effects could be much worse. Such issues are already a daily part of life in places like Las Vegas and Los Angeles. Both cities are within a very arid region, and neither has the natural resources to support a population of more than 25,000 people. Nonetheless, they have become the core cities in a megalopolis. Today, they have to bring water from hundreds of miles away to support their populations as well as the growing number of people moving into the area. They are expected to continue to grow over the next 50 years, and it will only become more difficult for these areas to support themselves in the coming years.

The problems we face today can't be the problems of tomorrow—if they are, they will have life-threatening results. But to meet the growing needs of tomorrow we'll have to envision and implement infrastructure in entirely new ways. This is only more reason to revisit the role humans play in nature, and to push green building toward a much bolder direction. If we can redefine our relationship with the environment, we may never have to worry about water or energy shortages again.

CHAPTER 7

WORKING WITH NATURE TO FIND CLEAN WATER

Water may cover 70 percent of the planet, but abundant and clean water is very much in danger of disappearing. In the United States today we use over 340 billion gallons of freshwater every day. Due to the way infrastructure works, it is not being replaced fast enough to keep pace. While green buildings have formulated ways to reduce the amount of water used, the infrastructure that delivers water to your faucet requires so much volume to operate that it negates any savings. Of all the issues that we will have to tackle in the future, water management is the one that showcases how unsustainable today's infrastructure is.

We will need to better understand where water comes from as well as where it can and cannot be found in sufficient quantity. Currently, all of society's apparatus for getting water to cities, towns, and people is geared solely to meet the needs of people. We do not share it, nor do we want to, it seems. An honest account of our designed world is that our approach to waterworks is harmful to the very supply we need. Solutions of tomorrow will have to minimize or altogether halt the inflicted damage we do. Surprisingly, we need only adhere to the rules water dictates via the laws of nature. By working with it rather than fighting against it we will find we can get what we want as well as learn to not always only take.

Figure 15 Example of how rivers are controlled throughout the United States, reducing the ecological value of water bodies. Credit: US Army Corps of Engineers

We have been very bad at protecting water resources during the past few centuries. Most people are not aware of how water operates in the natural world, and how it affects the ecology of everything around it. Just like us, all living things are dependent on water.

THE WATERSHED

Most of the time when we consider freshwater, we think of lakes, rivers, and streams that collect rainwater before they run into the ocean. The heat of the sun causes evaporation, creating clouds, and the whole cycle begins again. But this misses an essential piece of the process, namely *watersheds*. A watershed is fairly simple to understand. It is an area of land in which rain and snowmelt, known as runoff, drain across as it moves downhill toward an estuary, creek, river, or other water body. The more naturally covered the watershed is, say with trees, undergrowth, and grasses, the more the water naturally cleans itself. The less naturally covered it is with things

Figure 16 This image illustrates that naturally flowing water bodies do not typically run in a straight line. Credit: David Spencer, US Fish and Wildlife

like roads, parking lots, homes, airports, and the like, the more the water accumulates impurities like petroleum substances, fecal matter, herbicides, and fertilizers. Where soil is loose due to such activities as construction, agricultural activities, or removal of vegetation, erosion can occur.

The boundary of a watershed is determined by its drainage area. All rainfall that hits the ground inside the watershed boundary will drain into one specific stream. Any rain that falls outside the boundary will drain into a different stream. This threshold is infinitesimally thin. A dramatic and easy example to visualize is to imagine you are standing at the top of a peak in the Rocky Mountains. This is the Continental Divide of the United States, separating the watershed of the East from that of the West. Say you had a canteen full of aqua, and you unscrewed the top and poured its contents exactly at the dividing line; half of the water would drain west making its way to the Pacific Ocean, and the other half would drain eastward to the Gulf of Mexico and the Atlantic Ocean.

As the water from your canteen flows down the Rockies, it joins other trickles of water, eventually forming a stream. Other streams converge with still more streams to form small rivers, and then, in the largest watersheds, to form large rivers like the Mississippi.

Watersheds can be either large, continental-scale hydrologic units of area, or very small—just a few square miles or so, or even a small, unnamed trickle of a stream that may appear on the earth's surface only during the wettest periods of the year. The Mississippi Basin is the world's third-largest watershed (behind the Amazon in South America and the Congo in Africa), including 31 states and two Canadian provinces equaling around 40 percent of the landmass of the continental United States. Rivers like the Missouri bring water from as far west as Montana. The Ohio River forms a watershed that is approximately one-tenth that size, before joining with the Mississippi River. Two smaller rivers, the Allegheny and the Monongahela, each with a watershed of its own, converge at the tip of Pittsburgh, Pennsylvania, to form the Ohio River. Still smaller watersheds include those such as the Turtle Creek Watershed, which flows west from its source in Delmont, Pennsylvania, where it enters the Monongahela River. This smaller watershed drains an area of 147 square miles that includes forest, farmland, industry, abandoned mined lands, and urban and suburban communities—in total 33 different municipalities—and includes short streams like Dirty Camp Run, which is only three miles long. The Mississippi Basin brings water from Pittsburgh to New Orleans to the Gulf of Mexico within one huge water system.

In the case of the Mississippi, the cleanliness of all the main smaller drainage areas will ultimately determine the pollution within the largest one. For a hospital project I worked on in Monroeville, a town near Pittsburgh and situated in the Mississippi River Basin, we knew that how we designed the landscaping as well as parking areas and roof of the building would have a direct influence on the quality of water in nearby Turtle Creek, and as a result, the Gulf of Mexico. Nongreen, standard strategies are engineered to speed water runoff to a pond and retain it either for removal of pollutants or for more measured release into local surface water or groundwater.

THINKING LIKE THE WATERSHED

Our team chose to use innovative solutions like bioswales. A bioswale is a technique that uses vegetation, compost, or riprap—irregularly sized pieces of rock that are used to provide simple structure and stability—to naturally filter water. Bioswales slow the flow down so that particulates can separate during water's trip toward a holding pool. We also chose to use plants endemic to western Pennsylvania. When landscaping is not native, lots of pesticides and fertilizers are needed. In water systems, these foreign agents can kill fish, create algae blooms, and cause a host of other negative side effects. We estimated that the water from the project site was much cleaner than if we had gone with the status quo.

Even better, our clients now found themselves integrated into the natural world as the stewards for Dirty Camp Run and the Turtle Creek Watershed. It helped them communicate to the community that the new facility was not only a state-of-the-art healthcare facility but also a manifestation of how they wanted to assist in healing the nature surrounding them. By using bioswales at the hospital site, we mimicked the natural filtering process of vegetation in nature, but that is only one way that forests, meadows, wetlands, and other ecological conditions contribute to better water quality. One of the unseen, less obvious ways that watersheds affect water quality is through the falling of rain.

When it rains, some of the water makes its way into a stream channel fairly quickly—within a few minutes or hours. Some of the water will make its way to the stream channel in a matter of weeks, months, or a year or more. Yet some will never make its way to the stream channel at all. As rain falls, the soil on the surface goes from dry to moist as water collects and seeps into the soil. The wetter the soil becomes, the more saturated it is, and the more likely it is that the water will run downhill to a river or creek. Likewise, the steeper the slope, the more likely the water will run toward a body of water in a hurry, as opposed to seeping into the ground.

The rain that does enter the soil will become available to the root systems of things like trees, shrubs, and grasses, in turn strengthening the natural filtration capacity of the area. For that water, its journey ends by supporting the plant life, and then it will leave via evapotranspiration, the plant version of sweating. Back in the atmosphere, it will eventually fall as rain again somewhere.

But some of the rain will travel even deeper into the ground through soil and rock, in a process called *infiltration*. Infiltration is driven mostly by gravity, but the speed of infiltration also varies based on several factors that include frequency, duration, and intensity of rainfall, as well as the type of geological material it's moving through. Generally it tends to move about an inch per hour.[1] After traveling through the ground, as well as a completely saturated area of the subsurface known as the water table, it becomes groundwater. Groundwater exists within subsurface material such as sand and gravel, or within very porous or heavily fractured rock. A well drilled into it could pump a significant and useful quantity of water. A pool of groundwater is referred to as an aquifer.

Throughout this entire process, beginning with rainfall, continuing with infiltration through the soil, and eventually to recharging groundwater supplies, water quality improves. Plants and bacteria in the soil can remove bacterial impurities, while sediment and other impurities are removed by the natural filtration that the soil itself provides as the water moves downward through it. Sometimes the downward movement will stop after just a few feet where the water table is very close to the ground surface. In other, generally drier locations, the top of the water table is several hundred feet below the ground surface, which will require more energy to pump it to the surface for human use. But assuming that no additional pollutants are introduced into the subsurface, clean groundwater is an invaluable resource to supplying such needs as public drinking water and agricultural irrigation.

This is the process of water in all its flowing glory in a completely natural and undeveloped watershed. But as the Monroeville example hinted, a watershed malfunctions when human activity interferes. A watershed moves over artificial landscapes like parking lots, buildings, and sidewalks just as easily as it does across natural ones like forests, woodlands, and grass. Whenever we remove vegetation to create a strip mall, we remove a chief source of natural water-quality regulation. With the loss of vegetation, particularly by removing tree cover, we lose the network of root systems that helps the ground keep its structure, keeps slopes stable, and prevents erosion. These root systems also offer physical pathways that make it easier for water to infiltrate into and down through the soil. Remove the vegetation, and water is less able to enter the soil, resulting in increased runoff. Eroded soil, carried along by surface runoff, eventually makes its way to streams and rivers, where it degrades water clarity and quantity and negatively impacts the aquatic ecosystem, whose healthy functions depend on clean, clear water.

While the removal of trees and grass allows less water to seep into the subsurface, replacing trees and grass with buildings, roads, and parking lots allows none at all. A one-two punch occurs. First, the increased volume of runoff water will rapidly overwhelm streams—both the amount and the velocity of the water disrupt surrounding ecological systems. Second, since it is much more difficult for rainwater to reach the ground with parking lots on top of it, the groundwater is replenished at a much slower rate. Over time, the soil will experience too much evaporation and, taking into account the damage already done by the missing root structures, erode even faster. As rainfall rapidly flows along paved surfaces, it will pick up and carry along with it the chemical traces of our activities. The most obvious examples are distilled petroleum products like gasoline and motor oil and also the antifreeze that leaks from vehicles that give rise to these artificial hard surfaces.

An additional form of pollution that arises is *thermal pollution*.[2] Hard paved surfaces, often dark colored and fully exposed to sunlight, collect and store heat from the sun very effectively. When rain falls on these surfaces, it transfers that heat to the water. By the time all of this surface runoff makes its way to a stream channel, its temperature can be drastically elevated compared to the ambient temperature of the stream water. Just as aquatic ecosystems require certain conditions to remain stable and thriving, they require steady thermal conditions as well. Thermal pollution of waterways can result in a range of damaging impacts to an ecosystem that include decreased dissolved oxygen and nutrient supplies that aquatic life depend on, as well as disruption to reproduction.

For the better part of history, we did not have the scientific prowess to connect the dots. Only in the twentieth century did the term *watershed protection* enter our lexicon. Now we have a broad set of planning tools and protective measures we can take to keep damage from being inflicted upon the earth's precious freshwater. Watershed protection depends on expertise in the fields of geology, biology, ecology, and hydrology to determine the best techniques to call into action for a specific location. Where green buildings today are isolated into individual buildings, in tomorrow's world they will need to be more thoroughly and thoughtfully integrated into the natural world.

The work undertaken by the team for the Monroeville project could only influence the acreage of the site. Bioswales are extremely helpful in managing storm water on-site. But they are effective on a larger scale only if similar practices are used for all the other surrounding areas. The way that architectural projects are executed today is in relative isolation from other sites. If green strategies are to reach their full potential, the isolation of projects will need to be abandoned for more integrated approaches that tie all projects together. It will be some time before we see a new paradigm emerge because the use of bioswales is still unusual for buildings, but when they are used, projects can save money. Bioswales reduce the need for retention and detention ponds that hold storm water on-site during and after rain events. When correct types of flora are used, the runoff can be prefiltered before being released to natural bodies of water like lakes, oceans, and rivers. This means that oil, particulates, pollution, and sediment can be taken out before such foreign agents have the chance to cause problems downstream. Despite the fact that bioswales can reduce costs and preserve the environment, the technique is seen by many construction managers, civil engineers, and real estate developers as risky because it is not the standard way of dealing with storm water.

THE VALUE OF THE WATERSHED

One city that has learned to take advantage of its natural watershed is, perhaps surprisingly, New York City. It can cost between $100 million and $2 billion to build a state-of-the-art filtration facility. Once it is in operation, an army of workers is needed to maintain and keep it running smoothly. Filtering enough water to quench the needs of people can cost billions of dollars.

New York City does not spend a penny on filtration because it has instituted a vast number of measures to protect the watersheds of its water source. Just north of Manhattan, about an hour or so, you will find yourself in the thick wooded areas of the Croton Watershed spread across Westchester, Putnam, and Rockland Counties. It along with the Catskill/ Delaware Watershed provides 9 billion gallons of water to 8 million residents of New York City and other areas. Around 1,000 New York State Department of Environmental Protection employees live and work in the watershed communities as scientists, engineers, surveyors, and administrative professionals to perform critical jobs such as conducting more than 900 water quality tests daily to guarantee continual safety for those who will use it.[3] New York remains one of only five large cities in the United States that is not required to filter its drinking water.

The New York City water system is a more symbiotic relationship in which an ecological service has been preserved rather than edged out by buildings. The result is better quality of this fundamental component for human life. The economic benefit is that New York City saves billions of dollars each year. The healthiness of the reservoirs and watersheds guarantees quality aqua to millions of city dwellers. Many national surveys of the best-tasting water put the Big Apple high on the list. If you ask New Yorkers, they will tell you theirs is the best in the world.

PROTECTING THE WATERSHEDS

It's best to start watershed protection at the boundary line that defines a drainage area. Recall the example of the Continental Divide: water poured next to your left foot may find its way into the Colorado River and flow to the Gulf of California. Put away your canteen and have a look around you: what do you see to your left and to your right? Because you are on the Continental Divide, in the middle of the Rockies, you are most likely looking at some very steep slopes in either direction, but you are also looking at the beginning of the *headwaters* for watersheds to the east and to the west.

A watershed's headwaters are generally the most acutely sensitive to the effects of human activity. So to protect the watershed, we should aim for success at the headwaters. Generally, as at the Continental Divide, headwaters begin on steep slopes in most drainage basins. It is critical to avoid disturbing these zones in ways that decrease the amount of water seeping into soil or that increase runoff. Of course, this is easiest to do in pristine areas that have no development.

More often than not, however, watersheds and all their components (not just the headwaters, but wetlands, riparian zones that flank the stream channels, ground surfaces in the middle of a watershed at a distance both from the watershed boundary and from the stream channel, etc.) are long removed from their natural state due to agricultural activity and residential development. Agricultural activity requires repeatedly disturbing the soil, which increases the risk of soil erosion and sediment pollution. Industrial agriculture is based on the application of pesticides and fertilizers to create large yields of crop. Over time, this behavior can kill off the natural organic matter that combines with minerals to give the soil good structure, essentially chemically burning the soil, which makes it more easily removed by storm water.

The urban areas built before the beginning of the twentieth century were designed to move water as fast as possible into rivers, estuaries, streams, lakes, and oceans. These practices create thermal and chemical pollutions to these waters—it is why so many streams and rivers within urban areas are in bad shape. Other features like golf courses and lawns require the application of chemical fertilizers and pesticides to achieve the lush greenness we seek for them. When lawns and golf courses are placed within arid regions whose annual average rainfall could not possibly support the demand for water that they impose, they place both water quantity and quality stresses on a watershed.

A suite of techniques is available that can reduce or eliminate the impacts of our activities on watersheds. In agriculture, contour cropping—where rows are planted perpendicular to the slope of the land and follow the curves of the land surface, instead of being set up in long straight parallel lines that ignore topography—is a more sustainable option because it conforms to the topography of the land, helping to increase infiltration while minimizing runoff and erosion. For lawns, at a minimum the selection of less water-intensive, drought-resistant varieties of turf grass (best used in arid zones) is a good start. Native species can be used in place of a lawn altogether. Within cities, rivers, streams, estuaries, and lakes should be ribboned by wide easements designed to slow down storm water's approach to them from surface runoff. Large-scale bioswales are also a real option in some cases to divert and detain runoff to normalize water temperature, trap sediment, and remove oil and other chemical pollutants before they flow into the water system.

WATERTECH

A new arena of water protection is emerging. While it is not directly involved with watersheds, it does imitate them in important ways, and can be a viable option for protecting the water supply. Called watertech, it describes a group of innovations that couple water management with ecological functions.

Manny Papir is at the leading edge of watertech. He is the president of Aqua Sol Filtration Systems, which designs and builds water treatment systems that use no energy or chemicals. Papir's system, called Aqua Sol, has already treated billions of gallons of water that would otherwise have been lost as too polluted to reuse. Made of nothing more than hardy, native plants, the system can alleviate the burden of finding new water sources or over-pumping existing wells. He has partnered with a company in Europe to develop a water treatment system that imitates nature.

The Aqua Sol system is currently in use in more than 80 facilities. In Reus Airport, just south of Barcelona, the number of passengers increased from 500,000 in 1995 to 1.1 million in 2004, and by 2005 it had reached 1.4 million. This dramatically increased the outflow of wastewater from the airport, but the airport had no additional area for a new, larger waste system. Aqua Sol systems were installed, and today the airport has been able to handle a 150 percent increase in load, saving untold millions of dollars as well as eliminating any environmental damage that would have otherwise happened. Explaining the technical components does not do it justice. To see Aqua Sol constructed on a wetland or atop a retention pond resembles art more than engineering. The system is made of long, brightly colored ties that hold the plants in place. The placement of the plants is important because it allows for the density of the plants to be at a maximum level. As water interacts with the flora, it is cleaned through natural processes. After two to three years, you would not know if the water treatment system was a piece of nature or man-made.

Similar systems have been pioneered by biologist John Todd. His Eco-Machines can be housed within a greenhouse or a combination of exterior constructed wetlands. The system can also act as a water garden to be designed to provide advanced treatment. The Eco-Machine functions just like a natural system that breaks down waste entering the ecosystem, except that it is contained within individual tanks, creating independent treatment zones.

These types of solutions are ideal for urban waterways and industrial discharge in the green building of tomorrow. The benefits are enormous and have already saved millions of dollars while providing clean water. As megalopolises are developed more densely, unique solutions like these will be needed to retrofit existing city waterworks.

WATER BUDGETING

Solving the problem of water pollution is one side of the equation. The other side is availability. The rate at which society today is using water is depleting water resources upstream.

In tending to our personal affairs to keep ourselves adequately clothed, fed, and safely sheltered, we have to draw up and adhere to a budget. If we are careless, we find that our expenses outstrip our income. If this happens for a short period of time, we can recover. Over the long term, we will find that we can no long afford our lives due to debt and lack of money. Everyone knows about this from a financial point of view. We also need to start seeing water from the same perspective—something called *water budgeting*.

Hydrologists usually calculate the water budget for a specific watershed over a one-year period. Assume we are dealing with a small watershed that is always subjected to the exact same climatic and short-term weather conditions. We know through established weather records how much precipitation will fall. By mapping the land use within that watershed, the percentages of land area that is covered by forest, grasses, buildings, and pavement can be calculated. We can then calculate how much of that annual precipitation will evaporate and transpire, how much will be used by vegetation, how much will leave the watershed as stream flow, and, most importantly for us, how much will recharge groundwater. Those figures are matched to human activity to create a water budget. If we systemically use more water than the natural system can deliver, we end up with a very stressed system. Over time, wells go dry, stream flows decrease, and wider-ranging infrastructure is necessary to support the population. Not to mention all the ecological communities depending on the water that are also held in peril.

By calculating water budgets for individual buildings, we can work out the water budgets for several buildings and construct water budgets on neighborhood, community, and regional scales. By comparing the water budget for the natural system to the one for the human system, we will know if the community will outstrip its local water supply.

Unfortunately, when local water supplies prove inadequate, infrastructure has a habit of fixing its negative balance by finding more water somewhere else. Look no further than the number of golf courses surrounding Las Vegas or Phoenix, or, on a broader scale, the population of California, which is rapidly approaching 40 million, to reflect on water usage that is woefully out of whack with respect to the setting.

Before the Los Angeles area was settled by Americans, aboriginal people never numbered more than 25,000 in the area because the lack of water wouldn't support a larger population. In 1910, before the first major project was completed, fewer than 400,000 people lived in LA. In 1913, an aqueduct was constructed to bring water to the city from the Owens River, more than 200 miles away. A second aqueduct was completed in 1970, increasing the volume of water delivered to Los Angeles from remote locations by an additional 50 percent. Today, nearly 4.1 million people live in LA. New infrastructure projects are likely to be developed in the coming years to stretch even beyond the Owens River, but at some point nearly the entire proportion of southern California along with other water-starved places like Arizona, Nevada, and parts of Texas and Colorado will come face-to-face with the fact that their deficit of water has become a debt they cannot pay for with the old mentality of simply finding new resources to exploit.

Water budgeting is a new concept in the building industry—and not yet widely used for most projects. In fact, only one building standard calls for such a mentality toward design: the Living Building Challenge Standard. The Living Building Challenge Standard was created by the International Living Building Institute. The standard aims to advance sustainability by aligning buildings with the reality of limits and the goal of making society truly green. That translates into very forward-thinking concepts like water budgets that call for buildings to use only water that comes from captured precipitation such as rain and snow, or be part of a closed-loop water system that reuses water and does not use chemicals.[4] If a building is designed to be too big, in that it exceeds the natural supply, it would need to adjust to fit to the site, ecologically speaking. It also calls for managing all storm water on-site, so that it can only be released in a manner that would be in accordance with natural flows. Only a few projects, approximately 10 to 20, have used the standard; however, this is the direction all green buildings must take.

Instead of budgeting for water, we fill in the water gap through various engineered solutions, many of them extremely impressive in their own right. These bring water from hundreds of miles away and defer the imbalance for another generation of leaders. Environmental systems operate on very long time scales, so the water-imbalanced humanized systems can get by for a few decades, a blink of the eye in geologic time. But they cannot be sustained indefinitely. Many cities throughout the United States are facing the eerie reality that water somewhere else is not as readily available as once upon a time. As explained, most of the Southwest of the United States depends on waters from the Colorado River and Lake Mead, which was created by the installation of the Hoover Dam in 1935. It is the largest reservoir in the United States, and it extends upstream from the dam for more than 100 miles. The water in the reservoir and the power generated by the dam today serve up to 28 million people in an area whose population continues to grow rapidly. A combination of decade-long droughts and excessive usage has seen water levels drop 100 feet in Lake Mead. Las Vegas is embarking on a new billion-dollar pipeline project to bring water from even farther away. Authorities in the area have implemented water conservation standards for years, and they now admit that standard water efficiency techniques like gray water, low-flow fixtures, and not irrigating lawns are not enough to resolve their failing water supply. Sooner or later, they, and we, will need to learn how to live within our hydrological means on a consistent basis, and design, redesign, retool, and possibly vacate our existing cities, megalopolises, and buildings accordingly.

Learning to live within our environmental limits simultaneously poses us with challenges and presents us with wonderful opportunities. The financial and monetary constructs and rules that hold dominance over modern society do a terrible job of calculating the value of services that healthy natural systems provide to us through delivering the clean water and air that sustain us. This has often resulted in discounting them altogether when we draw up plans for buildings and supporting infrastructure. Today's economists have a keen interest in environmental and natural resource matters, and are making progress in translating natural services into financial terms. But with or without a solid monetary valuation, these natural ecological services are real, they are large, and even without our knowledge and understanding, our well-being is made possible through the value that they provide. Through rethinking buildings and infrastructure, with their natural limits in mind, we will become more attuned to the benefits that healthy, natural systems deliver. Healthy forests and burgeoning oyster beds offer a pair of examples to illustrate how and why this is the case.

FORESTS AS WATER SOURCES

A forest is a complex community comprised of varied species of trees of similarly varied ages, ranging from saplings to towering examples that stand 100 feet or more and have done so for a century or longer. A healthy forest will necessarily include all manner of nonplant life, ranging from mammals and fish down to the cellular scale of microbial life in the soil and water. Its diverse group of life-forms depend on one another for survival.

By the time European settlers arrived in the Americas, most of Europe's old-growth forests had been cut down as civilization established and spread, the trees used for masts, castles, arrows, and firewood. When the settlers began to arrive in North America in the seventeenth century, the new world that they found astonished them. The entire North American continent from the Atlantic shore clear across to the Mississippi River and beyond was completely covered with virgin, old-growth forest that had developed for the 10,000 years following the last ice age. Indigenous people had put their imprint on it, but to a scale that still made these lands virtually untouched by the activities of humankind.

Before long, the European settlers applied the same mentality and appetites to the new world. Today's remaining stands of ancient forest are a fraction of what they had been centuries ago, and they often exist in isolated pockets of diversity. The disconnection makes it difficult, if not altogether impossible, to support the highly varied network of species that once called the forest home. Only about 3 percent of Europe's ancient forests remain while in North America that value stands at below 30 percent. It is a pattern that is repeated wherever humanity has expanded and taken a foothold across the globe. Ancient forests were seen as a mere means to an end.

Today, trees are still often viewed as a commodity to sell, like wood or paper, or an obstacle to remove so a real estate developer can build new homes. Thankfully, trees are a renewable resource. Sustainable forestry—management of forests in a way that maintains the diversity and ecological services forests provide while extracting resources from them at a rate no greater than their natural ability to regenerate—is a growing trend. Much of what is called forest today is managed for our need for timber. And while in many such managed sites we can witness full stands of trees as far as the eye can see, they are pretty poor excuses for forests. A vast stand of one specific variety of tree such as Arkansas pine managed and grown for specific economic uses is a monoculture that does not have the full biological diversity of a forest.

Forests may cover only one-third of the land surface of the United States, but they process and deliver about two-thirds of our freshwater supply. Their thriving communities of plant life and mature, well-developed soils allow healthy forests to retain and store water, helping to mitigate against the risk of flooding and regulate surface water flows on a more measured and consistent basis. A vital, thriving forest provides shade that keeps temperatures in check and prevents unnecessary evaporation.

When we subject a healthy forest to industrial activity such as logging and building roads, we, not surprisingly, diminish their ability to regulate water. Without trees, less and less water is retained in the ground, leading to a diminished groundwater supply and an increased risk of flooding aboveground. In old-growth forests, a thick layer of decaying vegetative matter on the forest floor provides microbial and filtration activity that purifies water, but when trees are logged and not allowed to decay naturally, this important water-cleansing function is lost. The erosion caused by the loss of the trees' root structure to hold the soil together, as well as the activities of the loggers themselves, leads to sediment entering streams and rivers—polluting waterways at their source before they even make it downstream to us. The soil that erodes was specifically geared to sustain tree life, and it takes hundreds if not thousands of years to develop. Once it is gone, it is not coming back within our lifetime or within that of our children or their children.

The benefits forests provide are unimaginable to modern man but will be noticed once they are gone. The fraction of forests still in existence provides the backbone of all the water we drink and use. In the years to come, an investment of space to allow forests to naturally repopulate would pay for itself with crisp clean rivers and aquifers of water resembling those of the time before Europeans arrived. This is the hope for green buildings of tomorrow: not only that forest managers or landowners would engage in stewardship for forests, but that architects, engineers, and designers would be more interested in designing cities as old-growth forests, rather than turning old-growth forests into urbanized areas.

ESTUARINE SYSTEMS

Cities, megacities, and megalopolises are nearly always situated along coastal plains or other large bodies of water. They encroach on estuaries, unique aquatic environments that are found where rivers approach an ocean, which feature a mix of freshwater and saltwater and which are subjected to the movement of the tides. Many biologists consider estuaries among the most important ecosystem types on the planet, vital due to several reasons. They are the place that freshwater and saltwater meet—making unique niches for hardy species. The flora that grow within estuarine habitats, ranging in scale from microalgae to seagrasses, have been found to be enormously beneficial with sequestering carbon. Healthy estuaries can also provide protection to low-lying areas from storm surges and rising oceans.

Like forests, estuaries are equipped to benefit society as long as society does not negatively affect these ecosystems too much. One incredible example of this is with oysters. Many of us hear the word *oyster* and immediately think "delicious" and start looking around for the cocktail sauce and lemon wedges. But in their natural setting, oysters are a powerhouse machine of water filtration and purification. One individual adult oyster, in its process of deriving its nutrition from the water surrounding it, can filter up to 50 gallons of water per day. Upon the arrival of European settlers, the oyster beds in the Chesapeake Bay, off the coast of Maryland and Virginia, were vast and thriving and seemingly of infinite bounty. The oyster population in the 1600s was such that collectively, they could filter a volume of water equivalent to the entire Chesapeake Bay itself in about one week.

Over the past several generations, our appreciation of the oyster's deliciousness has outmuscled our understanding of its ecological value. Oyster fishing played a significant role in the economic vitality of the region as the country began to be settled, but harvesting activity over the generations has gone beyond the Chesapeake's capacity to provide them, a reality which would no doubt seem unthinkable to the area's early settlers.

Additional damage to estuaries is provided by activities far removed from the coastline. Agricultural activity and urban development have caused erosion and pollution, leading to severe water quality degradation of the rivers that drain into the Chesapeake. The increased sediment levels inhibit marine life's ability to absorb oxygen from the water, and other oxygen-depleting and toxic chemicals have made their way into the bay. The combination of overly aggressive harvesting with diminishing water quality has decimated the Chesapeake's oyster population, which further exacerbates degraded water quality through loss of their ability to filter and purify. For today's Chesapeake Bay oyster population, it takes about a full year to filter the same volume of water that centuries ago they could do in a week's time. But precisely as it is with forests that we choose to allow to regrow, so too can it be with degraded marine ecosystems. And with the oyster, we will find that by seeing to it that conditions permit them to thrive, we will have an ally in improving water quality. One place where this is happening is Withers Swash, a 4.2 square mile tidal watershed situated inside the city limits of Myrtle Beach, South Carolina, although standing at the edge of its estuary, you might not know that you are looking at a decades-long story of our irresponsible use of and relationship with water resources, as well as the future of how we will work together.

For the better part of the last 20,000 years, the waters of the watershed now known as Withers Swash have been rich with estuarine life like shrimp, crabs, aquatic grasses, herons, and oysters. The waters were clear and inviting. The banks and reefs of the basin were hatcheries for game fish that helped to keep the area stocked with natural prey. In fact, until about 1970, one day of fishing at Withers Swash could supply a week's worth of food for a family. Today, you would not want to eat anything from those waters, because Withers has become defunct with pollution from increased development and human activity. Community leaders, scientists, and designers, recognizing that the problems at Withers Swash cannot go on, are setting in motion a plan to return Withers to its once pristine condition with a particular eye on the oyster. With its impressive filtration and purification abilities, the oyster is the keystone species of the ecosystem, and its full reintroduction could orchestrate Withers' full recovery.

The community's approach to Withers incorporates three common techniques from conservation biology, a study within biology that focuses on protecting and preserving biodiversity and applying it to urban design. They are watershed protection, species reintroduction, and habitat restoration. Every ecologist worth his or her pay knows what these methods are, but few architects, engineers, real estate developers, or designers use these tools on a daily basis. However, these three areas encapsulate what needs to be done in the green buildings of tomorrow. When strategies such as these are the central focus of construction projects in the future, we will find working solutions to common problems with water quality within cities and in nature before they get away from us and do long-term harm to the systems that sustain us.

The work in Withers Swash, spearheaded by a community collaborative as well as nearby universities and businesses, started in 2008 with the introduction of the first oyster reef. One reef can be home to thousands of

Figure 17 View of Withers Estuary. Credit: Neil Chambers

oysters, making it a reliable water filtration system. The goal is to intro-
duce new reefs each year as well as grow awareness of how community-
based efforts can restore the area.

Withers Swash is not the first to use these techniques. In Jacksonville,
North Carolina, similar practices are being used on Wilson Bay. Wilson
Bay was once so degraded that residents avoided its waters. It got so bad
that, in 1998, the local government, concerned with wastewater being
pumped into the bay, shut down the facility. The city could find no precedent to clean up the mess within a water body as big as Wilson Bay,
measuring 106 acres. The city asked Jay Levine, a North Carolina State
University College of Veterinary Medicine researcher, for ideas. Levine
had studied oysters produced through aquaculture techniques in France
and created a strategy based on reintroducing oysters as well as clams and

Figure 18 This image shows how oyster reefs are reintroduced into Withers Estuary to form the basis for repopulating oysters and improving water quality. Credit: Neil Chambers

mussels back into the waters to enhance water flow and dissolved oxygen levels.[5] He and his colleagues used several techniques to help ensure the new marine life took hold in Wilson Bay, and soon the water quality began to improve and ecological features reappeared. Only two years into the project, ducks came back. Soon after that, golden eagles and ospreys appeared.

Tomorrow's green building techniques will see projects such as these move forward on a massive scale. Architects and designers are not thinking about oysters or ecological systems in any serious way yet. But the problems of tomorrow will challenge the profession to reevaluate what green really means. After all, that is how water works.

CHAPTER 8

ENERGY BETTER SIZED

Buildings are energy hogs, and the energy sources that power them, like coal and natural gas, are killing us and the environment through widespread pollution. Add to that the energy used to create building materials, and it's a real mess. But the biggest consumer of energy is the infrastructure that brings electricity from the coal plant to our homes and offices.

The electrical grid's transmission lines lose a whopping 65 to 70 percent of the electricity created before it even reaches us. Just to get enough juice to run factories, houses, and traffic lights means producing nearly 200 percent more energy than needed. The additional output from power plants means more pollution and more problems. As a result, many people are calling for a smart grid. The smart grid is what energy experts say we need for the next generation of power delivery. It would replace the current transmission lines constructed with superconductive materials—so that at normal temperatures no electricity would escape. The smart grid would also use a more intelligent meter to keep track of all electricity flowing in the system at all times. The grid would communicate with appliances inside homes and offices to determine the best times for things like washing machines and air conditioners to run at the lowest cost to the consumer. Such plans are being proposed in the United States and other countries. A supersmart grid has been proposed for Middle East, Europe, northern Africa, and Turkey that would connect all of these regions with an extensive smart power grid. With the deserts of northern Africa ideal for solar power generation, the idea is to use the region as an energy depot for all of these nations while implementing smart technologies to regulate usability and electric flow.

Smart grids are an important component for all countries wanting to establish utility scale renewable energy sources. In the United States, as in Europe and Africa, some areas are best for wind power (like the Great Plains), while others are good for solar (such as the Mojave Desert), while yet others (like the coast of California and the eastern seaboard) are best suited for wind, tidal, and wave power. If the Alliance for Climate Protection has its way, it would see the Mojave Desert carpeted with a solar array 96 miles by 96 miles in breadth. Likewise, the plains in Middle America are ideal for wind power because they are mainly flat and treeless. Imagine a bucket of water being tossed at a screen door. When the water hits the screen, it would go in all directions, though most of it would go through the screen. Wind acts the same way. As it hits objects, it shatters. The more vegetation and buildings a gust of wind hits, the more uneven it becomes. For wind turbines to work the best, you want direct bursts of air currents perpendicular to the blades. Very few obstacles present themselves along the prairies. This makes them ideal, second only to offshore wind farms. Offshore wind farms located a few miles off a coast have nothing standing in the way of wind turbines and the wind itself.

There are a few problems with the smart grid and utility scale renewable energies. One is that by placing solar farms and wind power in places where they function best, the energy generation is moved even farther away from the end user than with current practices. Renewable energies also generate electricity intermittently. That means they are not continually producing energy, nor can you control or rev up production as needed. It has to be sunny for solar panels to absorb sunlight and breezy for turbines to turn to create electricity. This is not the way people use energy. In the morning and during the day, cities are awake with activity, computers are turned on, office lights are glowing, televisions are playing, and people are moving throughout buildings. Energy is at a high demand. It is also in high demand later in the evening, but not as much. And then at night most people are asleep—and with them, so are TVs, ceiling fans, laptops, and microwaves. So energy is not in demand at all. But the wind could be blowing, and electricity could be getting made. The electricity is sent to the grid, filling it up with new power, but there is nowhere for it to go. In theory, the smart grid would have the ability to store it, so as the morning comes back, and people begin to crawl from their beds to meet the dawn (and maybe the wind is no longer blowing), they could still use their hair dryers, ovens, blenders, and anything else they need before they race off to work or school.

Many government officials and green leaders believe such a modernized electricity network is the best chance we have to address energy independence and global warming. Unfortunately, it advocates the same mentality regarding infrastructure that we currently have. It should be big, inflexible, centralized, and permanent. Hi-tech solutions are prone to breaking down. The smart grid would be costly to update, upgrade, and maintain, meaning the efficiency would begin lagging shortly after it was completed. If fixes are too inordinate, people quickly revert to doing what is cheapest and fastest. This would undo any good that the smart grid had done. Plus, updating the transmission lines with superconductive materials is currently too expensive and not available for mass installation. To upgrade the transmission systems throughout the United States would cost over $2 trillion or $100 billion over the next 20 years.[1] Once up, they could prove to be twice as efficient as what we have now. However, the materials to make them are still scarce, making such a project more theory than reality.

Large utility scale renewable projects create big problems of their own. It does not matter whether the renewable source is wind, solar, or biofuel; they all take up massive chunks of land. By sprawling over the landscape they have negative consequences on every ecosystem they encounter. Habitats are undermined. Natural water systems are overly impacted, and ecological services are interrupted. It has been estimated that the amount of land needed for utility scale wind, solar, and biofuel production will be larger than the state of Minnesota—about 80,000 square miles.

These considerations bring the topic to a specific point. Only two choices exist: the future of energy can either be more effective or stay ineffective. Big, centralized, and inflexible energy sources are ineffective. They sound very cool and have lots of bells and whistles—but they are not good for the environment. We will not be able to regrow old-growth forests that would provide the carbon sink the atmosphere needs. We would not be able to benefit from the improved ecological services like better air and water quality. We would have wind and solar power, but we would lose the potential for greater advances. Large-scale renewable energy projects focus on creating more energy to meet demand. Focusing attention solely on capacity overlooks the greatest resource for energy savings—buildings.

BUILDINGS THAT CREATE THEIR OWN ENERGY

The beauty of some renewable energy sources is that they can work outside of the context of enormous centralized power plants. In the case of solar panels, you can have your energy as part of the building. When solar panels are integrated into the roof and walls of a building, there is no need for transmission lines or a smart grid. The energy supply is directly connected to the building. Where zero loss is impossible with utility scale renewable projects, it is much more feasible with building integrated photovoltaic panels, which are known within the green design community as BIPV, and on-site energy generation. BIPV are panels that are built into the building. This is a smart approach for renewable energy installation because such a method reduces the cost associated with purchasing solar panels. For example, solar panels are a very good material to use as roofing. Instead of constructing a roof and then putting solar panels on top of it, BIPV cuts out the unnecessary conventional roof for a roof that generates power, is better insulated, and cuts down on electricity bills.

In 2000, I worked on the Stillwell Avenue Subway Terminal, in Coney Island, New York. The station was first built in 1918, but by 1998, it was in need of a major renovation. We designed the train shed to use 76,000 square feet of solar panels as its roof in three arching spans that allowed exposure to the sun throughout the day and the year. In all, the roof consists of 2,730 panels and provides a comfortable area for passengers as they wait for the train to take them to Manhattan. The total amount of energy generated was 250,000 kilowatt-hours per year. Assuming an average home consumes around 1,500 kilowatt-hours a year, you can figure out how many homes could be powered with the technology. At its completion in 2004, it was still one of the largest solar panel building installations in the world. Today, it is hardly considered big.

In 2010 alone, four massive solar panel projects were under way worldwide, in total creating more than 16 megawatts of power. These projects generate more than 75 times the amount of energy of the Stillwell Avenue project. The largest of these multi-megawatt projects is the newly built Hongqiao railway station, located in Shanghai, China. It is a 6.7 megawatts installation with the capacity to make more than 8 million kilowatt-hours of electricity each year, or the equivalent of that used by 5,500 houses. Since then, the Chinese government has contracted another 13 solar projects like the Hongqiao project and committed to installing 20 gigawatts of solar energy capacity by 2020. If they achieve their goal, the solar energy can potentially serve nearly 17 million homes each year. Building integrated solar panels are not like other renewable energy sources. The benefit of solar panels being built into the structure means energy is consumed where it is produced. This makes for much smaller losses with transmitting electricity from a wind farm or coal plant hundreds of miles away. Other benefits include that no additional land is required for energy production. Plus, a roof made from solar panels will last 10 to 20 times longer than conventional roofs. You do not need to improve the energy grid with a smart grid that is expensive and hard to manage.

Other types of on-site renewable energy sources include vertical axis wind turbines. These are smaller versions of the more familiar horizontal axis turbines. Vertical axis systems stand only about 125 feet tall, around the height of a ten-story building. The wind turbines that are being planned to overpopulate the Great Plains are five to six times that height. The larger a turbine is, the more effective each rotation is, which means more electricity per cycle, but they can't be sited close to buildings or cities. Large wind turbines can also be dangerous. They commonly break when wind speeds and wind shear overwhelm them. You can find an assortment of videos on youtube.com that show just how violent it is when a 500-foot-tall spinning windmill crashes under the pressure of gale air currents. Vertical axis turbines are far less deadly and do not have the same reach as their bigger counterparts. They also function in low-velocity winds, whereas the larger turbines need faster wind speeds to turn. Small-scale wind projects can be sited nearby or on-site. As with the use of solar panels, the closeness of the end user means that less electricity is lost and no upgrades to the existing grid are necessary. And neither solar panels nor turbines need to use an acre of wilderness because they can be situated within cities or megalopolises or on buildings.

Surprisingly, biofuels can also be on-site energy sources, and they can even be used with regular generators. Not all bioenergy sources are created the same, however. You have ethanol, flex fuels, biodiesel, and algae. Each is made from different processes, and each takes a different amount of energy to produce. Likewise, each has a different energy output when used. For example, ethanol made from sugar and corn is typically so high-energy intensive that it takes more to produce it than it provides during usage. The other big problem with corn- and sugar-based fuels is that growing the crops requires additional acreage. This means more natural lands are turned into agricultural fields, more water is diverted to nourish them, and more chemicals are used to grow them. In the end, the environmental impact is huge, and the benefits are none. Flex fuels are nothing more than gasoline mixed with corn ethanol. It is packaged and sold to people as an alternative to regular gasoline. But it comes with all the same problems petroleum products bring along with all the ecological damage from ethanol. Many people consider it the worst of both worlds.

The ideal situation is to have on-site energy generation with fuels that take up no natural lands, need no water, and produce more energy than was needed to create them. Waste to fuel is a practice that is fairly old news in the green world, and now many green companies are reinventing the concept for modern uses. The practice of reusing cooking oils for biodiesel buses goes back as far as the 1960s.

For nearly 20 years, Aaron Levinthal provided power via large generators to hundreds of outdoor concerts and festivals. The generators were always set up as far as possible from the event due to the smell and smoke that comes from standard petroleum-based fuels. The motors would bellow a thick black cloud of noxious fumes from the moment they were cranked up to the moment they were shut off. For years, he was told that there was no alternative to petroleum-based diesel. His self-driven desire to find the answer set him on a path to discover an alternative. When he first found out about biofuel, everyone continued to say that it could not be used, that it would destroy his equipment, and that it was more expensive. Instead of listening to them he created B100, a fuel derived from soybean shells, which would otherwise end up in a landfill. Over the last ten years, he eliminated all use of petroleum. Levinthal told me that so many people had bad experiences with the petroleum generators that it took some of his clients several times of using the different fuel to believe they did not have the same results.

One of the drawbacks of biodiesel is the time it takes to make it. Yet that is changing too. Onsite Energy Company, in Flint, Michigan, has partnered with a local community college to develop the Genesee Biodiesel Processor, which can use virgin or used cooking oil along with methanol and other ingredients to produce biofuel in a matter of hours. The company is targeting school districts, farmers, and local government as the source of things like used fryer oils and other waste products that can serve as the raw ingredients. Once the fuel is created, the company could provide it back at a reduced rate to help bring down the cost of transportation. If technologies such as these become the standard way of dealing with waste products, biodiesel will provide a real alternative to expensive and centralized infrastructure.

Smaller is better when it comes to energy production. Society is no longer as stationary as it once was—and it is useful to be able to take down your energy generator and take it with you. On-site generation such as solar panels can be deconstructed and moved. Communities can create a cooperative to build an on-site energy generation and then cluster homes and work spaces around the technology. If governments were to invest in small projects such as these, there would be less outlay of capital than for one gigantic project.

SAVING ENERGY ONE BUILDING AT A TIME

Replacing one energy source for another does not reduce the demand for energy from buildings. Energy efficiency is also needed. Current techniques and methods could reduce building energy demand by 80 percent. Energy used to manufacture building material could easily see a reduction of 50 to 60 percent. As the amount of energy is driven down by efficiencies, less electricity would need to be created. If a home needs only 20 percent of what a conventional house needs, on-site energy production would be 80 percent more affordable. It is important to make sure that any solution that can improve efficiency does not create bigger problems. A technology that is suggested as a way to meet the goal of improving performance should always be subjected to a life-cycle analysis. As discussed earlier in the text, a well-established suggestion for people to go green is by replacing incandescent lightbulbs with compact fluorescent lightbulbs, or CFLs. Energy Star explains that "if every home in America replaced just one incandescent light bulb with a qualified CFL, in one year it would save enough energy to light more than 3 million homes."[2] It sounds almost too good to be true: you just go out and buy a CFL bulb, screw it into your lamp, and you are saving money and energy. However, the story does not end there. The new technology may deal with one problem, but it creates a much larger one.

CFLs contain mercury, which is a potential human health issue. Mercury acts as a neurotoxin, interfering with the brain and nervous system, and can be particularly hazardous for pregnant women and small children. Prenatal and infant mercury exposure can cause mental retardation, cerebral palsy, deafness, and blindness. Even in low doses, mercury may affect a child's development, delaying walking and talking, shortening attention span, and causing learning disabilities. In adults, mercury poisoning can adversely affect fertility and blood pressure regulation and can cause memory loss, tremors, vision loss, and numbness of the fingers and toes. Evidence also suggests that exposure to mercury may lead to heart disease.[3] Many generic brands of the light fixture have been known to short-circuit and begin to burn while still screwed into a light socket. As you unscrew them, they break, releasing the mercury inside of them. Many green advocates have downplayed the mercury the CFLs contain because each bulb contains only a small amount, about four milligrams. It is true, one CFL is not dangerous, but we will not be dealing with only one over the next few years. Here are a couple of things to know: A lethal dose for an adult is about 1,000 times what is contained in a single CFL (approximately 1 to 4 grams). However, half a gram is enough to warrant a fish advisory warning for a 10-acre lake. In looking at just one lightbulb, there is no reason to worry, however. The EPA estimates that nearly 300 million CFL bulbs were sold in 2007, and that 14 percent of the mercury contained within the bulbs was released into the environment. That means that almost 200,000 grams of mercury was released into the environment from CFLs in 2007 alone.[4] That is enough to warrant a fish advisory warning for a lake the size of Lake Michigan.

Sales of CFLs in 2007 were only about 20 percent of the market. If everyone starts to use them, nearly 1.5 billion would be sold each year—adding about 1,500 pounds of mercury into our homes and the environment. Many countries around the world are outlawing incandescent lightbulbs. Cuba outlawed them in 2005, the United Kingdom will no longer use them by 2011, and Canada will stop using them by 2012. States such as

California are expecting to phase out incandescents by 2018. The phaseout of incandescent bulbs leaves CFLs as the most affordable alternative.

On NPR's *All Things Considered,* John Skinner, executive director of the Solid Waste Association of North America, explained that companies and the federal government do not have an effective way to have Americans recycle or dispose of the energy-efficient bulbs correctly. He makes it clear that a problem with the bulbs is that they break before they reach the landfill—for example, in the containers, Dumpsters, and trucks on the way. This puts workers at high risk of exposure to large amounts of mercury. He added that when bulbs break near homes, they can contaminate soil.[5] This is the same soil that makes up the yards in which pets and children play.

This is another case of a solution causing more problems. Trading human and ecological health for the sake of short-term solutions will only make people distrust real progress and make it harder to accomplish. It is not enough to call a product green just to add to the bottom line.

Better approaches are available, but they are not as easy to implement. A preferable way to reduce energy demand in buildings is to reduce the need for artificial light. Artificial lighting is a substantial consumer of energy. In places such as offices and retail spaces, it can account for as much as 50 percent of electricity consumption. Buildings that have large floor plans have to have lights turned on throughout the day. The excess heat generated by nonnatural lighting means additional energy has to be used for cooling.

Mandatory levels of daylight would greatly lower the electricity used. Daylight alone cannot always provide enough light for complete comfort, but it is a real option without negative side effects. A good start would be to update the EPAct to include mandatory levels of daylight within all buildings. Some countries already call for such requirements. Daylight is not new, but to require it would be. Techniques have been around for centuries to improve the quality of daylight coming indoors. In my experience, architects have for a long time designed for natural light from the point of view of emotion. They rarely test their ideas to show quantitative results. This is changing, but not fast enough. Many green buildings have daylight as a feature; coupled with on-site renewable energy sources, they could soon create all of their own energy.

Natural ventilation is another way to save on energy. Natural ventilation is designing buildings to allow for airflow to move throughout spaces. This isn't possible in all climates, such as the Southeast of the United States, where high levels of humidity could spell trouble in the form of mold and mildew in ductwork and on walls. It also depends on the type of building as well as the type of interior space if natural ventilation can be used 100 percent of the time or only partially. In the United Kingdom, natural ventilation has become a staple with buildings. Integrated Environmental Solutions, a company from Scotland, developed software to help engineers and designers quantify the benefits for clients. The software takes out the guesswork for building projects. Clients get to see through simulations of interior space just how much fresh air is available with a design that is coupled with dollars saved by using natural ventilation.

THE CHASM BETWEEN BUILDINGS AND THE NATURAL WORLD

For green building to deal with the problems of energy is one thing. For them to deal with it while restoring the natural world is something completely different. The green building industry is focused on buildings mainly because that is how real estate developers, architects, and engineers think about projects as well as how property rights, site limits, and boundaries dictate scope and magnitude. In the future, entire cities will have to be retrofitted, not with better windows or lightbulbs, but with buildings, infrastructure, and systems that adhere to climatic and ecological realities.

Urban areas are much more complex than a single building. The increasing number of people living and working within megalopolises complicates the situation even more. Within a megalopolis is a matrix of support services allowing for everything from ease of transportation to economic engines to energy/power delivery and waterworks plus waste management. Globally, there are more than 2 billion buildings, not to mention all the infrastructure that goes along with them. Simple ways to green a building are available, but simplicity can miss the point. Solutions need to get much more involved if they are going to include issues such as habitat restoration, watershed protection, and protection of species.

In short, a huge chasm exists today between green building and ecological sustainability. While architects and city planners are the ones who design our megalopolises, only conservation biologists are looking at issues of ecological and land management at that scale. Vast wilderness is the only system that matches the intensity of megalopolises. The sheer size of an ecosystem can dwarf that of multiple metropolitan areas, megacities, and towns. Yet it is the patterns created by cities, highways, buildings, and other human structures that are typically the dominating feature within immense landscapes—the eye follows the line created by a road slicing through a forest while trees blur into a mass of green. All biologists can cite lists of predicaments the built environment has caused living sciences, but most collect data within their chosen field, as if you can keep the human world and nature separated.

This is a problem for scientists such as Dr. Reed Noss, director of the Science and Planning in Conservation Ecology lab at the University of Central Florida, located in Orlando, Florida, which serves over 56,000 students. He believes the human world and nature must intermingle with each other. According to Noss, planners are not versed in biology. They do not understand that not all land is equal. Some land has a higher potential for biodiversity. Currently, although real estate developers may be aware of species on sites, there is no financial incentive to leave pristine lands alone. Noss wants to change that and intertwine architecture with ecology. He has spent much of his recent career evaluating and analyzing fragmented wildlands in Florida. Noss's goal was to identify lands that are good for habitat and also had other viable habitats close to them. Florida is one of the most developed states in the United States. As a peninsula, it depends on energy being trucked in, usually in the form of petroleum, natural gas, and coal. The fact that the state is a peninsula with a narrow profile east to west makes lands fragile, even before the fragmentation of natural habitats by roads and subdivisions, because species are blocked by large bodies of water to the east, west, and south. Florida's widespread development, as well as its fragile ecosystems, meant, as Noss puts it, that neither ecologists nor designers can work in a vacuum.

What he helped to do was to bridge the gap with a program called Florida Forever, a blueprint for conserving natural resources. Since its inception in July 2001, it has acquired more than 2.4 million acres. The project focused on saving strategic habitats that contain rare species, including over 620 sites that are home to nearly 600 rare, threatened, and endangered species. The program also incorporated nature trails, bike paths, and greenways (areas such as old train tracks repurposed for recreational walking), fragile coastline, functional wetlands, sustainable forestland, and archaeological and historic sites. The basic concept is to lace fragmented land together to create corridors for wildlife to move freely. With access to different areas of the state via these pathways, animals can commingle in order to establish new genetic highways—offering the potential for more biodiversity and large populations of healthy species.

Noss also notes that highways and subdivisions are a grave danger to many animals. The Florida puma nearly went extinct because of collisions with cars. This is a problem not just in Florida. Nationwide more than 400 million animals become roadkill each year. This is mainly the result of highways, interstates, and roads being placed throughout wilderness with no understanding of what is there, or what habitats were being divided or separated by the construction. For example, connection to essential mating or hunting areas can be cut off by an eight-lane freeway. When this happens, animals have little choice but to cross the highway. Collisions with cars are inevitable, which put both the animals and motorists at risk for injury. In the case of animals, death is the usual result. Often people are killed too, or severely hurt, as well as property being destroyed.

Human society has a strange love/hate relationship with nature. We love to peer out a window at it…or hike within it…we love the idea of saving it, but we do not want to have it determine our fate. The law of the wild is not the law of man—for most of our civilized history, we have seen nature as nonhuman. The fight between ecology and technology is pitting ancient nature against innovation. It need not be a fight. Ecomimicry is a natural next step. In the same way that airplanes must adhere to the laws of aerodynamics, so too must society adhere to the laws of ecosystems. The success of Noss in Florida shows that we can make the built environment an extension of nature as we marry the disciplines of architecture and conservation biology. In fact, in some ways the Forever Florida program is a move toward becoming more of a keystone species. We are acting like the beaver in a sense. Where beavers build dams and abandon them, we are removing blockages such as roads and buildings to permanently reconnect habitat. When looking at a map of the conservation work happening in the Sunshine State, the land purchased is often beside a larger piece of federal or state-owned land. This expands the habitat of any species in the area. Once less ecologically significant lands are determined, buildings could be developed on them. Often, this is at the outskirts of natural areas.

Couple this type of design process with old-growth forests, oyster restoration, and watershed protection, and a matrix of ecological services within the context of human society begins to emerge. Nature and urban areas become more closely tied together. Nature has more land, humans have less dependence on ineffective infrastructure, and buildings are set to take another step toward complete integration with nature. We will not have to leave technology behind to do this; it is just that we will have to trust ecology more. And this brings back the question of big infrastructure or small sources for energy generation. Big infrastructure is not equipped to engage natural lands in a positive way. Huge grids allow development to simply spring up in distant lands or in the middle of strategically important habitat; you just have to plug into it. Power

Figure 19 Before and After: This beaver dam was removed by dynamite, illustrating the strength of beaver construction. Credit: US Fish and Wildlife Service

companies are like any other companies; they need to keep growing customers. So for them, they would rather keep their inflexible modes of operation to enhance users. But on-site generation, namely solar power, is ideal for coupling with projects like Florida Forever. As lands are identified as either high- or low-value habitat, roadways and development can be incentivized to use the less valuable ecologically rich areas. This could work the same for watershed protection and old-growth forests, but on a much larger scale. For old-growth forests, they need not just small patches of land, but a widespread territory that could encompass parts of multiple states and/or provinces. The wildlife corridors would be innate to such hydrological features along with the many ecological services provided. And the most important innovation paving the way for this ecomimicry world to come into reality is also one of the most surprising.

THE FUTURE OF POWER

On-site, compact energy is an essential element for ecomimicry. The major reason is that such a power source would free up a tremendous amount of land currently used for transmission lines and power plants.

It would also mean we would not need large-scale wind farms or solar arrays that carpet fragile ecosystems. Hydrogen power is the ultimate on-site, cheap, and effective energy source. In the past, hydrogen was too expensive to create on a large scale. In fact, if viewed from the perspective of big infrastructure, it will be too expensive for another 200 years. But a new smaller infrastructure, called micro-infrastructure, could both help reestablish forested areas and drive development. It could also give people control of their own power supply by eliminating big power companies. One nice thing about hydrogen power is that the only emission is water vapor. How does it work? It is pretty simple. Hydrogen is made of two parts: a proton and an electron. When you feed the hydrogen atoms into a fuel cell, they split into protons and electrons. The electrons move in one direction and protons in a different direction. The electrons create an electrical charge, which creates electricity. On the other side, the hydrogen re-forms with oxygen to create water. Water is also a great source of hydrogen, and an electrolyzer can easily do the job of separating them. But until recently, this took more energy than it created, similar to the case with corn ethanol. The equipment that could split the hydrogen efficiently was not yet mass-produced and was thereby very expensive. All that has changed, the hydrogen economy having dawned.

Three factors are working to bring about this revolution for hydrogen that can change the way we think about green buildings, energy production, and, ultimately, ecomimicry. With on-site energy generation now, you have to have a large roof for solar panels, or you need to have biofuel generators. Though the generators produce 80 percent less emissions, imagine an entire city with its own generator. Issues of fuel supply and pollution could still be a slight problem. With hydrogen, a fuel cell needed for all the energy needs of a house would be no bigger than a closet, and the fuel source could easily be rainwater collected. Only two by-products occur from the process of hydrogen energy generation: one is water vapor and the other is oxygen. Every house in America could have a fuel cell feed with rainwater and powering everything from the toaster to computers to televisions to recharging mobile smartphones. You would have to buy the fuel cell and a few other components. Once turned on, energy would be absolutely free. Having this independent access to in-house, clean, renewable, nontoxic energy would eliminate the need for other sources. No more coal plants, no more natural gas, and no more gasoline. No need for a smart grid or high-tech transmission lines. There would be no need for the electrical grid.

Fuel cells have never been made at a quality that would bring down their cost. However, the growing interest in alternative fuel cars has sparked a competition between major automobile makers to be the first to offer hydrogen-fueled cars to the mass public. Hydrogen cars are a much better option than plug-in e-cars because they don't rely on grid-based energy and can be made without burning coal and without large infrastructure.

Figure 20 Example of beaver architecture, intertwined with natural surroundings. Credit: US Fish and Wildlife Service

Chemist and professor Daniel Nocera, along with his associates at the Massachusetts Institute of Technology, has found a technique to make hydrogen from water with inexpensive and widely available materials.[6] The technology, called Sun Catalytix, splits water into oxygen and hydrogen fuel, mimicking photosynthesis, meaning only sunlight is necessary for the process to work. The basic components are similar to those used in photovoltaic panels. Nocera's invention could be the basis for new storage systems that would allow buildings to be completely independent and self-sustaining with regard to energy: the only energy input would need to come from daylight or wind to create hydrogen fuel. As the fuel is created, a fuel cell would use it, or it would be used by another device or devices to produce electricity or transportation fuels as needed.[7] In fact, such large solar panel projects like the ones in China or Coney Island could power electrolyzers with excess energy from the solar panels. As Nocera's technology comes to market, clusters of buildings throughout a megalopolis could be powered by a source as benign as a swimming pool of water.

California has developed plans for the hydrogen highway. The original idea was to build hydrogen fueling stations from Sacramento to San Diego that would give motorists using hydrogen-powered cars the ability to drive the entire distance and refuel. These fueling stations would look similar to normal stations except they would have hydrogen instead of gasoline. The hydrogen could easily be created on-site, unlike conventional fuels such as gasoline. With gasoline, first oil must be extracted from the earth, processed to create gasoline, and then transported across the planet by ships and trucks to gas stations so that you can fill up your tank for several dollars a gallon. The environmental impact of moving oil from place to place as well as processing it is high along with the emissions that come from using it in automobiles.

The planners of the hydrogen highway began to recognize that most drivers do not normally drive from Sacramento to San Diego on a daily basis—a more than 500-mile trip. The plan, which was developed by the

National Hydrogen Association, began to see that the best way to encourage people to experiment with hydrogen cars is to create a cluster of hydrogen stations starting in two cities: Los Angeles and San Francisco. Then, as more hydrogen-powered cars are available within the area, the stations can branch out following demand. The National Hydrogen Association is a membership organization founded by a group of ten industry, university, research, and small business members in 1989. Today the group has grown to over 100 members, including representatives from the automobile industry; the fuel cell industry; aerospace; federal, state, and local government; energy providers; and many other industry stakeholders. Several car companies, including Honda and GM, have offered select customers the opportunity to lease or own hydrogen prototypes within areas of existing hydrogen fueling stations. The number of hydrogen cars on the road has been pretty small since the beginning of the program, which started in 2008 to 2010. That will change over the next decade. Automotive companies like Mercedes-Benz, BMW, Kia, and others are all rolling out fuel cell cars. Mercedes has already begun to offer a large number of its F-Cell (between 50 and 200) to people living in Los Angeles and throughout Germany. Drivers will lease the F-Cell for two years, and then testing will be performed on the cars to see how regular wear and tear has affected the technology. As more hydrogen cars are released into the market by automotive companies, the price will fall and other uses for small-scale fuel cells will be available.

Soon, the same hydrogen systems within the cars could be mass-produced and used for other purposes, meaning creative designers will retool them for buildings at an affordable rate. The most economical way to implement hydrogen is not with big infrastructure but with giving every house and building its own system, or building networks of between 10 and 30 houses that rely on a larger fuel cell. At this scale, both in size and in cost, nearly everyone can afford it. The implications are huge. Neighborhoods with houses that have lost value could come together to install a hydrogen power source to drive up values. With only a small upfront investment, entire communities and towns could begin generating easy-to-install hydrogen systems for their residences. Excess hydrogen could be supplied to fueling stations to sell to the growing number of hydrogen motorists getting on the road.

This is not science fiction. The cluster concept already has a pilot program in Denmark. On the island of Lolland, the fourth largest of the country, the Danish Energy Authority in a joint partnership between the city, IRD Fuel Cells, and Baltic Sea Solutions started creating hydrogen from excess wind energy for five homes in 2008. They were given a fuel cell the size of a small central heating unit to convert the element into electricity. In 2009, the project expanded to include another 35 houses. By 2012, all 40 households will be completely powered with hydrogen. Denmark is not the only place where there are hydrogen-powered houses. Currently there are two such residences in New York and New Jersey as well as a 400-kilowatt fuel cell in New Haven, Connecticut, that is the largest stand-alone renewable energy generator in an apartment complex anywhere in the world.

Fuel cells are the ultimate on-site energy source. The new growth of megawatt solar panels means that entire cities can be self-sustaining without the need for external energy sources. And the more an area clusters close together, the more effectively hydrogen sources can deliver. This will help lead urban areas to become more densely populated. If this technology can be combined with projects such as Florida Forever, regional development could be driven by decisions for conserving biological life and ecosystem functionality. As fragile areas are identified, infrastructure causing problems with connectivity could be removed and habitats could be repaired. Large-scale infrastructure today is presented to people as if it is a necessity, but it is not. Big systems cost lots of money to maintain and operate. It is very hard to remove something like a coal power plant or thousand-acre wind farm once it is established. And those that own them will want to keep people using the energy they are selling. But this way of thinking is outside the framework of restoring ecosystems, reconnecting fragmented lands, and giving people what is needed in the least harmful ways. These are the green building principles bubbling to the surface today, and they will most likely be used in developing the guidelines for green buildings in the future. Such a mentality would relieve the troubles facing the watersheds and habitats that provide us with clean water and so much more.

CHAPTER 9

BRIDGING THE DIVIDE BETWEEN BUILDINGS AND WILDERNESS

Our society will not transform into a more ecologically friendly society overnight, but it is already under way. Over the next several decades, the gap between nature and urban space will narrow. Problems with energy efficiency and energy creation are not going away anytime soon; nor will the difficulties surrounding water shortage go away. The effects on the environment from the manufacturing of building materials along with the construction of buildings will continue to be harmful.

The most common goal in developing ideas for today's sustainability movement is to not be as inefficient as existing methods, or at best, to be net neutral (meaning that any harm to the environment, such as that caused by driving a car to and from work each day, is offset by something that mitigates the specific harm caused). Net neutral, like many things within the green industry, is usually defined by a limited set of criteria. A good example is with carbon emissions. Say Person A uses energy from the grid that is made from coal. The coal emits carbon during the making of electricity. If Person A decides to plant enough trees that will take the same amount of carbon out of the atmosphere that was created by generating the energy he used, that is considered net neutral. Buildings can work the same way. If a building has a solar panel array installed on the roof that during the winter generates only 80 percent of the energy it needs, it will have to get the other 20 percent from somewhere else. Most likely that will be from the electrical grid, and as was the case with the first example, the electrical grid's energy is made from coal. But if the solar panel system generates 120 percent of the energy it needs during the summer, the building can sell that extra 20 percent of energy back to the grid, offsetting its use of the grid energy in the wintertime, and thereby making its annual carbon impact net neutral. Of course, this doesn't take into consideration all of the environmental harm done by using coal, such as mining, transporting, and preparing it to be burned to create electricity. The way we calculate the carbon impact of coal does not reflect the other impacts associated with each step.

No perfect answer is out there to eliminate every single impact that comes from living on the planet. But that is the beauty of keystone species. Beavers, who are unsustainable in the short term, are also so integrated into the ecological functions of an area that they benefit the forests and all the life that surrounds them. Dr. Clive Jones, a terrestrial ecologist and senior scientist at the Cary Institute of Ecosystem Studies, a world-renowned organization in applied ecology addressing some of society's most pressing problems and based in Millbrook, New York, believes that humans can also learn to be keystone species, or what he likes to call ecosystem engineers. Ecosystem engineers are like keystone species except that ecosystem engineers typically modify habitats. Oysters, which, as discussed in Chapter 7, are an important keystone species, are not ecosystem engineers, while beavers are. Jones thinks that people could contribute as much positive impact to the richness of regions as beavers. Like us, beavers have a big ecological footprint on the habitats they are in. Their dams flood large areas, and they clear-cut woody plants for construction and food. One family of beavers can easily modify several acres of land. If other beaver families live in the same area, they collectively can have a dramatic and overarching influence on everything from the amount of oxygen in the water to what trees grow to what bird and predator species survive. Yet, the disruption of water flow and the damming of streams that beavers cause overall have a positive effect. Jones's research compares the diversity of a stream where beaver dams have been built to that of a free-flowing stream. What he found was that more biodiversity existed where dams had been built. However, there are winners and losers. Fish that are accustomed to fast-flowing water do not do well in waters slowed by blockages of sticks and leaves. Plants that prefer drier conditions can be eliminated from riverbanks, where the soil turned up by the construction of beaver dams is saturated. Thus, even though beavers are vital for the eco-health of a forest, they can negatively influence other species.

But that is not the end of the story. Because beavers do not take over the entire habitat of a species such as a trout, which likes fast-paced waters, these fish can continue to thrive in areas where beavers do not build dams. So in that way a perfect balance is struck. Beaver dams encourage increased biodiversity along streams. In other areas of the same ecosystem, streams not affected by beavers are home to those species that do not like what beavers do. This balance supports a larger range of species than if beavers occupied all the streams, or if there were no beavers at all. It is a win/win situation.

Similar patterns appear when humans modify the environment with buildings. Some animals do thrive in more simplified conditions, like those of a city or suburb. Deer and crows are two species that prefer the open, field-like conditions of suburbs. In cities, cockroaches could not exist in colder climates if not for heated homes and buildings, and populations of rats are so numerous in settled locales only because of the number of food scraps people throw away. There are primary differences between the modifications made by beavers and by humans. One is the scale on which the two species modify nature. The other is the fact that when beavers run out of readily available trees, they move on and allow their former home to fall into disrepair. When humans build buildings, they stay put.

Both Jones and Richard Noss, whom we met in Chapter 8, point out that the biggest problem caused by the built environment is not carbon emissions but fragmentation of habitat. Studies show that many animals can adapt to climate change if it is slow enough. Pioneers in the science of genetic ecology have found that if a species (plant or animal) has the

Figure 21   This interchange illustrates how highways and roadways separate and fragment natural areas. Credit: US Fish and Wildlife Service

opportunity to cycle through four generations during a climatic shift, the species can typically adapt to the modification of the environment. Estimations from climate experts show that temperature and weather pattern changes are slow enough for many species to adapt to.

But species can't adapt to losing habitat. Or it should be said that some animals can't. Species are geared to specific conditions within their surroundings. They have acquired the attributes over long periods of time during their evolution. Take a fish out of water, and it dies. It sounds obvious, but it illustrates the point. Fish have evolved for the habitat of water. And not just any water. Some fish like cold water while others like it hot. Some like it deep while others like it shallow. The same is true for land animals. Beavers have adapted to chew trees, and are better adapted to forested lands. As they make their ponds and lodges, these things act as a barrier between them and their predators such as wolves and bears. Put a beaver in a pond, and you will have a hard time catching it. Put it in the middle of a parking lot, and you will have little trouble running it down. Beavers are hardwired for woody places with streams. They need space, and because the way they build their dams is unsustainable, they need places to go after they abandon them. Fragmentation of the habitat hinders that movement.

Subdivisions simplify the biodiversity with grassy lawns, driveways, and ornamental flora. Factor in a few busy intersections with traffic lights and cars, and a beaver has no chance of surviving. Nor do a list of other species. They are living in pieces of the original forest. Where once they may have been connected by a wide stream, they are divided by parking lots, overpasses, and restaurant franchises. Reassembling the habitat into a cohesive unit that then connects to vast wildernesses at the scale of Yellowstone or the Great Plains is the best chance for sustaining as many living organisms as possible. Vastness is necessary for the health of all species, including people. With vast wildernesses, watersheds can work correctly, ecosystems can be restored to provide ecological services, and all living things benefit. Moreover, vast wilderness is more likely to provide the framework for thousands of niches that overlap with one another, creating unique opportunities for evolution and biodiversity. But to get to that place, planners and scientists have to find ways to conserve and reconnect the fragments of nature that still exist.

In Florida, the Everglades restoration proves a strong example of how to reconnect fragmented lands. These large projects serve as ecological reserve design, or eco-reserve. The restoration of the Everglades in Florida has been ongoing since the 1990s, and it is a prime example of how ecological services can be reinstated even after years of being nearly dismantled. Moreover, the Everglades restoration is not happening in distant lands far from civilization. Key cities and tourist destinations like Miami, Fort Lauderdale, West Palm Beach, and Key West are within the boundaries of the Everglades.

In the late 1800s, the Everglades started in the middle of the state, just south of Orlando along a narrow strip of land where the meandering Kissimmee River creates a floodplain that feeds into Lake Okeechobee. The lake covers about 730 square miles, which is around half the size of Rhode Island. As the waters flow south from the lake, it forms a slow-moving river 60 miles wide and over 100 miles long made of sawgrass and marsh supported atop a shelf of limestone. By the time it drops into Florida Bay at the tip of the state, the Everglades encompass the entire southern portion of Florida. During the wet seasons, the network of marshes experience flooding, and in dry periods they are stricken with drought. Such features offer tremendous water storage for neighboring communities as well as a natural hydrology that can prefilter the resource.

The Everglades of the 1890s, however, were considered nothing more than swamp and wastelands that could be put to better use. And by 1890, the vast watershed was being drained to make way for homesteads and farms. By the mid-1900s, efforts were redoubled to build thousands miles of canals, levees, and water control devices to speed the drainage for even more development. Overseen by the Army Corp of Engineers, the extensive network of civil construction redirected and choked the flow of the main rivers, cut off large chucks of wetlands, and replaced natural lands with homes, businesses, and agriculture. In a span of 50 years, the vast river of grass had been reduced by 50 percent. Instead of sawgrass marshes and cypress swamps that created habitats for possum, alligator, bobcat, fish, heron, and white-tail deer, there were roads, concrete, dikes, and buildings. The channelization of the Everglades began to serve as the groundwork for what would become the waterworks for southern Florida, delivering needed drinkable water from Lake Okeechobee to the major cities like Miami and West Palm Beach. Crops of sugarcane covered 440,000 acres of the Everglades, or approximately 27 percent of the habitat. Another 60,000 acres used to grow more traditional vegetables as a winter food source due to the warm year-round climate. Engineers channeled and straightened the Kissimmee River in an attempt to control flooding in areas that were being developed. The result was that 40,000 acres of wetland dried out.

As more water receded, cities and ports like Miami and Palm Beach grew bigger. Railways and roads were built as each new township grew. A recurring pattern emerged—more people moved into the area, so more offices, houses, roads, and commercial spaces were built, which attracted more people, and so more land was drained. The pattern supported a population explosion. In 1900, only about 1,000 people lived in Miami. By 1920, the Miami metropolitan area was home to over 66,000 people.

Figure 22   Drainage ditches like this one in the Florida Everglades were used to divert water flow, which led to habitat disappearance and water quality problems. Credit: US Fish and Wildlife Service

The Sunshine State's population grew from 270,000 in 1880, before the Everglades' waters were rerouted, to nearly a million by 1920—most of whom settled within the boundaries of the former marshland. Today, over 30 percent of Florida's residents live in the Miami metropolitan area and another 10 percent live in Orlando—both formerly part of the Everglades.

In the mid-1960s, problems began to surface. Algae blooms began appearing throughout the remaining streams and swamps of Florida, as a result of phosphorus, an additive to soil to help sugarcane grow, and runoff and waste from dairy farms. The Kissimmee River, now altered and straightened, brought huge amounts of nitrogen and phosphorus into Lake Okeechobee, resulting in an algae bloom in 1986 that covered one-fifth of its area. The additional phosphorus also created problems for wildlife. The high level of nutrients altered the growth patterns of cattails so that they became thicker and more compact. This prevented native birds and alligators from nesting within them. Without available spots, the species were not able to lay eggs. Their numbers started to dwindle.

Power plants creating energy for new houses and buildings leaked mercury that entered the environment as rain and dust. As a consequence, mercury levels in fish became so high that signs were posted to warn fishermen of the potential threat of contamination. Nearly 90 percent of the original waterfowl disappeared from the Everglades as a result of the contaminated fish, and runoff from the tip of the state caused coral reefs to be damaged throughout the Florida Keys. Populations of largemouth bass dropped, while the number of heron, egrets, and wood storks were cut by two-thirds. Another 69 species, including the Florida panther, were listed as threatened or endangered by the state and federal government.

So much water was sucked from the Everglades that it lowered the water table of the region and contributed to brush fires and sinkholes. Because of the state's peninsular geography, Florida's low-lying aquifers also became susceptible to saltwater contamination. If ocean water seeps into the underground wells, it takes thousands of years for the damage to be reversed. Many coastal wells are already experiencing this type of contamination, and have been for a number of years. If water usage continues as it is today, Florida will have no credible source of freshwater for the millions of people living and visiting there.

Even before the ecological importance of the Everglades was understood, forward-thinking citizens created grassroots campaigns and organizations, which helped to protect the remaining areas of the Everglades. They saw the beauty of the Everglades disappearing because of the creation of new farms and housing developments. They wanted to stop the destruction before it was too late. In 1934 the Everglades National Park was established, saving 25 percent of the original ecosystem. Today, it is still the third-largest national park in the continental United States, after Death Valley in California and Yellowstone. Only 45 miles west of Miami is the northern border of the Everglades National Park. Farther north, in Palm Beach County, is the Arthur R. Marshall Loxahatchee National

Wildlife Refuge. The refuge was established in 1951 under the authority of the Migratory Bird Conservation Act and is the last remnant of the northernmost area of the Everglades. The refuge totals more than 145,000 acres of habitat and is maintained to provide water storage and flood control.

Around the time that the parks were formed in the Everglades, grassroots organizations began to lobby for a comprehensive revitalization of all remaining areas of the ecosystem. For decades, citizens in partnership with officials, conservation groups, universities, and others worked to kick-start the project. In the 1990s, a serious restoration of the Everglades finally got under way. Federal, state, and local governments along with the Army Corp of Engineers, nonprofit groups, and businesses established the Comprehensive Everglades Restoration Plan. The plan predominantly focuses on the Everglades' role in the watershed it occupies, which has the potential to supply an average 1.7 billion gallons of water a day. The plan was to recharge underground aquifers and wetlands. Such measures can ensure reliable freshwater resources well into the future. To balance the needs of urbanization and ecological necessities, 80 percent of the water would stay within the environment. Some of the water would recharge aquifers. The rest would be allowed to spread across the Glades to keep wetlands thriving. About 20 percent would go to surrounding cities, towns, and other communities. Over time, better water management would help to restock fisheries throughout the coastal areas of Florida and the Gulf of Mexico, along with improving recreation and tourism. As the wetlands become healthier, the Everglades would provide storm surge protection for low-lying cities and developments.

The focus on restoration has already shown improvement for urban areas. Water quality has consistently gotten better, reducing the amount of treatment the water supply needs before it is safe for consumption. As marsh and wetlands are restored, rivers dechanneled, and habitats rehabilitated, fish and birds return. Today nearly 350 bird species have been identified in Everglades National Park. Of those, new populations of wood stork, great blue heron, great white heron, and snowy egrets have been established, and more than 100 freshwater fish have been documented during the last ten years.[1] In addition, regulations have been set on power production in the region, which has helped to reduce mercury levels, though some areas are still highly polluted.

The Kissimmee River revitalization project, which began in 1997, is proof of the potential of ecological improvements to benefit both urban areas and biodiversity. Engineers, designers, and scientists have restored headwaters once choked by canals and dikes. Important wildlife like pink-tipped smartweed, horsetail, sedges, rushes, arrowhead, duck potato, and pickerel weed have returned. The new force of the river has pushed out aquatic weeds that were deterring growth and life. Sandbars have reemerged. Cypress and other trees are growing back. The mix of flooding, species, and flow rates has intensified levels of dissolved oxygen in the water, while offering new niches crucial for crayfish, shrimp, and insects. The presence of these invertebrates increases the number of fish, birds, and other aquatic predators present in the habitat. The Kissimmee River revitalization is considered to be the largest true ecosystem restoration project in the world, attracting ecologists from across the United States and abroad. It is also testament to how ecological services can work only when partnerships are created between science, engineering, and public and private parties.

Even better, for some, was that the restoration of the Everglades turned out to be hugely profitable. A report released in 2010 by the non-profit Everglades Foundation described the return on investment from the comprehensive plan to be more than 400 percent in the coming decades. Projections in the study indicated a possible additional 442,644 jobs over the next 50 years. The US Army Corps of Engineers also estimated that an additional 22,966 new short- to mid-term governmental jobs would be created as a result of the restoration projects. The study goes on to show that the original investment of $11.5 billion could return an economic benefit of about $46.5 billion, and up to $123.9 billion during the duration of the project.

Today, the project faces new challenges. The highest point within the Everglades is approximately three feet above sea level. If the predicted

Figure 23 After restoration of the Everglades was undertaken, habitat re-emerged throughout previously disturbed areas. Credit: US Fish and Wildlife Service

sea-level rise from global warming happens, nearly all of it will be inun-dated. For species like the Florida panther, higher waters could mean losing a quarter of its habitat. According to Dan Kimball, the superin-tendent of Everglades National Park, these new issues make restoring the Everglades even more important. If the flow rates are reconstituted, they could actually help fight back sea-level encroachment. The stronger freshwater would push against the ocean to keep saltwater from pouring into the park and developed areas. "The best thing we can do to stave off climate change is do everything we can to restore a natural landscape," says Kimball. This would save countless homes and businesses, and prove to be well worth the costs of revitalizing the ecosystem while saving bil-lions of dollars of revenue for Florida.

Eco-reserves are a comprehensive eco-conservation strategy for pro-tection and restoration of biological integrity throughout a region. The current practices within architecture have grown out of a perspective that believed people were fundamentally different from other species. Its cur-rent forms do not protect or prevent the erosion of ecology. Ecological reserves try to step in as a break to stop ecosystems from further eroding. In examples like Florida Forever, the matrix of corridors and open lands allow for a complete array of all native ecosystem types and successional stages across the natural range of variation. In other words, all eco-zones and biodiversity are represented because all niches where species live have been saved. This, in turn, allows viable populations of all these native spe-cies throughout individual habitats and adjacent areas to be maintained in abundance.[2] In essence, it is recreating the way a fully intact ecosystem would work if human disruption has not occurred.

Three main components go into designing an eco-reserve: core reserve, corridors, and buffer zones. As explained by Dr. Stephen Trombulak of Middlebury College, these are the dimensions and levels that must be combined to form the full scope of biological integrity. The primary goal is for the ecological reserve to buffer large core areas of land and/or water while giving wildlife the ability to connect through its entire range—be it a few acres or a few hundred million acres. This is the only way to maintain a balance in which organisms are able to adapt to changes in their environment. The core reserve is the central feature of the design. Core reserves are either large swaths of the environment that have very little fragmentation and/or highly valuable habitat. Situated around the core are buffer zones. A buffer zone can be a piece of land that is used to soften a transition from a more hardscape condition like that of a road, neighborhood, or city. In some cases, you can have an inner and an outer buffer zone, depending on the fragility of the core area. If you were standing in front of a buffer zone, it might look like a group of trees in a park or a lightly used recreational area, seasonal picnic area, or campground in a national park. These buffers provide ecological protection for core areas while separating the natural lands and human development enough to allow people and wildlife to go about their business safely and without interacting. Also, the buffer can be the delineation of where more modification to the natural lands starts and stops. Inner buffer zones are typically less modified by human activity than outer buffer zones. On large-scale projects, services such as eco-forestry, a sustainable way of managing and harvesting timber for products, can be incorporated into the inner buffer zone. The outer buffer can be farmland, orchards, some types of housing, and other low-impact development as long as it is not too intrusive on the environment.

The protection of a single core area is not ideal, because one individual piece of land acts as an island isolating everything within it from any other area. It is better to identify two cores that are close together and connect them with wildlife corridors. Corridors are a tricky design item for eco-reserves, because different species require corridors of different widths and various criteria. For example, most herd animals like buffalo or pronghorns will not pass through choke points or under anything that they can't see to the other side. With wildlife corridors, isolated populations of species are able to reconnect with one another, increasing the size of the gene pool. For many endangered species, connecting fragments of wilderness together can mean the difference between extinction and survival. If a network of eco-reserves can be set throughout developed areas as well as connected to bigger wild areas, biodiversity could spring back to life.

Buildings block the wilderness corridors that would allow local migration from inland to coastal plains. If we could plan our cities and suburbs in a way that allowed the corridors to remain intact, we would do wonders for the environment and help ensure that a wide diversity of species continues to exist throughout the United States. This is an important point because most megalopolises are situated along a coastal area or close to a large body of water. They stand in the way of the coastline, acting as one giant blockage. Remembering back, grizzly bears serve the function of transferring oceanic nutrients inland in big amounts. Megalopolises hinder the same thing from happening because they block the coastline from the inland wilderness.

Over the next few decades, urbanized areas will expand and become more developed and more highly traveled. Highways, cities, commercial zones, and residential areas all contribute to the fragmentation of the natural world. If we want to avoid further harm to ecological services, we have to find ways to enable species to move from one area to another in relative safety. Finding ingenious ways to establish wilderness corridors is the next big problem green buildings need to tackle.

The beaver is unsustainable only over the short term. Over the long term, it is a keystone eco-engineer—generating the force and direction of entire forests. But beavers are unable to permanently transform an ecosystem, and instead modify only a few acres for a short time. This is where humans fall short. We have to replace the idea of having permanent buildings and cities with more ephemeral spaces—or as Clive Jones put it, "How do you make a building that changes all the time?"[3]

I do not think we will start making buildings from mud and sticks. I also do not think we will start abandoning our houses periodically, only to come back a year or so later to rebuild it. But there are examples of people abandoning civilizations. The ruins in Central and South America reveal that people have walked away from massive settlements in the past. When people leave, any nature that is left will cover nearly all signs of monuments and dwellings. But if they have damaged the environment too heavily, sometimes it can't recover. That is what happened with the developments of the Anasazi of the Southwest. The deforestation was so complete that still, many years later, the woodlands have not recovered.

Another example of this is Easter Island. Easter Island is a Polynesian island in the southeastern Pacific Ocean, most famous for its 887 extant monumental statues, called moai. These sculptures were created by the early Rapanui people. When the Rapanui people first found the island around A.D. 400, the island was heavily forested with a unique array of species. Over the next few centuries, the settlers deforested the land and overused the resources such as trees and natural food sources. The depletion of trees caused soil erosion, making it impossible for any vegetation to grow back and farming difficult. The population crashed, and in the late 1800s Europeans brought infectious diseases that wiped out most of the remaining people. Though very few people live on Easter Island today, the forests have not recovered, and they will most likely never recover on their own. Transforming ourselves from anti-keystone species to keystone species will allow modern civilization to avoid damaging nature in the same way. Society can begin to build a legacy of restoration and rebirth for Earth.

CLEANTECH

Cleantech is an industry growing at a supersonic speed. Anything that deals with energy, water, and green buildings fits into the market. Billions of dollars are invested in cleantech companies every year. The smart grid is a cleantech innovation; so is the software by Integrated Environmental Solutions. Hydrogen cars, Sun Catalytix, recycled particleboard, and fly ash concrete all fit into the world of cleantech. New innovations such as smart meters that regulate how much energy your house uses are also part of cleantech. As was suggested earlier in the text, industries like cleantech and greentech are red-hot with activity and finding innovative solutions. Cleantech has a strong network of organizations and companies participating in all areas, from energy generation to waste management to water purification, to bring products and services to market. At events like the Cleantech Forum, held in California, New York, and Europe, start-up companies can pitch their ideas to venture capitalists and corporation giants such as Morgan Stanley, Autodesk, and Deutsche Bank. This sector will only get hotter as China, the United States, and Europe commit more funding and attention to developing renewable energy and energy efficiency. The small businesses of today that are creating products to get funded will be the technologies of tomorrow that the rest of the world will be buying to improve energy efficiency. Unfortunately, these companies are still primarily concerned with finding purely technological solutions to today's problems instead of engaging ecology as an answer. It is unclear if the solutions these innovators are finding today will have a positive net effect on the environment.

There is not as yet an industry that focuses on how ecological services can be improved via interaction with design and development. Life-cycle issues are still not at the forefront of most professionals' minds, and it may be another ten years before the design world has the tools that will enable it to address pollution and inefficiency throughout all aspects of the building process. With manufacturing representing 50 percent of all energy used globally, this is an aspect of green building that deserves real attention in the coming years. Software does exist to calculate the life cycle of some products, but it is hard to understand and not easy to use. It was created for highly technical people within the area of life-cycle engineering. What is needed is software that can be used by designers that gives them the tools to make the best possible choices in future projects. Seamless integration into the design process will take time to create. Even when that happens, explaining the financial benefits of life-cycle analysis will prove challenging. Unlike energy efficiencies that save energy during operations, life-cycle savings happen before anyone steps into a building. If a product reduces the energy required for its manufacture by 75 percent, how does that translate to consumers? The savings will be somewhat invisible to end users unless the green building community is able to explain it to them.

PASSIVE HOUSE AND THE FUTURE OF CONSERVING ENERGY

Along with cleantech, another design method is finding a real foothold. Prefabrication, also known as prefab, is a new idea of how to build homes. Most people are used to seeing construction crews making walls and roofs on the construction site. Prefab buildings are milled in a factory setting just like a car or any other product would be. Doing it this way eliminates the human error of on-site construction and makes the walls more energy efficient. One group of prefab buildings, called Passive House, is a standard of home construction that has shown great energy savings. Passive Houses use superinsulated walls along with prefabricated building components to ensure they perform at the highest level possible. Completed projects easily save 75 percent to 80 percent compared to average houses. The first was built in Germany in 1990, and since then more than 25,000 have been constructed across Europe. The United States has been slow to adopt the approach, and there are currently no more than 20 in the country. One of those, a Passive House near Bemidji, Minnesota, uses 85 percent less energy than a house built to the Minnesota building code.

It may take some time for Passive Houses to make inroads in the United States. In Europe, Passive Houses are still about 5 percent more expensive than other dwellings, and in the United States they can be as much as 15 percent more expensive. In the future, Passive Houses could be produced just like any other mass-produced product, and this would make the homes less expensive. Moreover, they are much more energy efficient than the standard green building—which means more savings. This also means that on-site energy generation can more easily become the sole electricity required.

Prefab houses, hydrogen power, and Passive Houses have to mature as an option before they will become affordable. I believe that the next few years will see that happen, as people better understand how the three can work together to bring down costs. If you look at the pattern of green buildings being built in America, it is only a matter of time before the costs of Passive Houses are reduced and the structures can be more readily built.

Lower costs for innovative design will allow for green designers to achieve another goal: that of zero energy buildings. Zero energy buildings create all their own energy without ever needing energy from the grid, or as mentioned above, they create more energy than they need and can feed that back to the grid. If creative developers or designers were to use solar panels to produce hydrogen, they could quickly create a large enough supply of hydrogen to fuel a development of houses. They would be completely independent of the energy grid, and would foster a real world guide for a new way of thinking and building micro-infrastructure.

Efficiency, however, can't be a means unto itself. If we compare how cars improved fuel efficiency from 1950 to today, it becomes clear that efficiency can create more pollution than it solves.[4] As motorists were able to go farther with less gasoline, automobiles became cheaper to own. Plus the materials used to construct vehicles got lighter and lighter, which again improved their gas mileage and reduced the cost of the sticker price. Over time, cars became more compact as well as more affordable. What happened was that more cars were sold, and thereby more cars were on the road. From 1960 to 2007, the Research and Innovative Technology Administration of the US Department of Transportation (USDOT) reported that registered passenger vehicles more than doubled from 61.7 million to 135.9 million vehicles.[5] More telling is that the USDOT reported that from 1970 to 2007 the national average of miles driven tripled.[6] The result was that all the associated problems from cars increased, and though less gas was being used per mile of travel, the overall effect was that there were more carbon emissions than ever before.[7]

ONE STEP CLOSER TO BEING A KEYSTONE SPECIES

Passive Houses, like green buildings in general, do not engage nature. They take up as much land as all other buildings. Ecological sustainability is nearly absent from the approach of such innovations. At present the only time that such projects incorporate ecological sustainability is with green roofs and living walls.

Like many green features, green roofs and living walls are not new. They have been around for centuries but have seen a tremendous amount of activity during the last 40 to 50 years in Europe and now in the United States. At their essence, these architectural features are roofs and walls planted with vegetation. People love green roofs and living walls. Of all the green features embraced by the general public over the last decade, nothing has been met with more fanfare. They are built throughout the world from large-scale projects, such as the 450,000 square foot green roof atop the Ford Motor Company's River Rouge Plant, in Dearborn, Michigan, and the vertical garden occupying the exterior walls of the Quai Branly Museum in Paris. In some cases, a green roof is installed without any of the other features of green buildings being part of the project.

Green roofs have many benefits, including reducing runoff from a building site, as the vegetation holds rain longer than a normal roof. They also can lengthen the life span of structural systems by eliminating heat from the sun and ultraviolet light from directly striking them. The living wall of the Quai Branly Museum is wildly popular. Most pedestrians can't walk past it without staring at it. It stands nearly 50 feet tall between a wall of glass paneling and the exterior of the classically styled museum build-ing. The vegetation envelops the museum wall in an explosion of greens and browns along with an array of textures and shapes. The vertical wall of plants is interrupted only by large square windows that puncture the plants like a reminder to onlookers that it is part of a building and not a majestic hillside in the country.

In the past, such treatment of architecture would be a disaster. Roots and water would penetrate the surface, causing leaks and pest problems. In the case of the museum, the designer, Patrick Blanc, used a unique system that prevents these problems. It is made up of three parts: a PVC layer, felt, and a metal frame. No soil is necessary, so it is very light to the point that it can be suspended in air. The plants grow freely and carpet the surfaces without any of the negative effects that can cause water damage or prob-lems with cracking. Similar systems are used for green roofs. There is a ready-made system that includes the plant material along with soil inside a tray that comes with seedlings. These systems come to a site and are placed onto the roof very easily and quickly. Another type is a do-it-yourself system. You first have to apply a membrane to the roof. Once the membrane is in place, soil is added atop it and then vegetation is planted.

Blanc is famous for his vertical gardens that are both indoors and outdoors, on walls and on ceilings. Another of his projects in New York City occupies the top floor of a spa at Fifty-eighth Street and Lexington Avenue. From the street, the greenery is visible through large plate glass windows as if a giant plant has overtaken the building but is trapped inside with no way out. It has a tremendous presence and provides a deeper story about how humans are still disconnected from nature even as greenery is added to buildings. However, these types of installations are only great ways of imagining what the next step could and should be for green roofs. Currently, architecture leaves roofs atop a building with no interaction with the ground, but if the forms of buildings were designed to take in more daylight or create better natural ventilation, the four walls and roof aesthetic could be dismantled. Green roofs would have the ability to escape onto the walls and then the earth, stretching toward other buildings. Imagine a suburb designed as a buffer zone where the houses act more as a way to soften the neighborhood's edge against a forested area than as the edge itself that needs softening.

Both green roofs and living walls are beautiful, but Clive Jones says they are not the same as a complex community of plants and animals on the ground with the dynamic of an ecosystem. These designs do not have the same level of biodiversity found in natural landscapes, nor are they connected to the earth in ways that extend habitat, which is work that is desperately needed to preserve biodiversity. They are mainly ornamental, and because of that they are missing the juiciness created when ecological features overlap to form unique environments.

Green roofs are, at best, a starting point to reimagine the urban landscape for the century to come. They will need to move away from being isolated architectural details and start engaging the earth in a more fruitful way. Perhaps the next generation of green roofs will be designed not by architects but by urban designers and planners in partnership with ecologists and conservation biologists. Or maybe there will be no designer at all, and biologists will design the essential parts of our future cities.

At the outskirts of a megalopolis, core areas of eco-reserve could be created. Throughout England, green areas have been preserved to provide access for people to nature. The practice is known as a greenbelt. Greenbelts are areas that municipalities have set aside to try to limit growth of a city or town. Toronto, Ontario, has a hotly disputed greenbelt that one day could function as an eco-reserve at the edge of the major Canadian city. Portland, Oregon, is famous for the green ring around its city that offers a buffer between city life and nature. The negative side to greenbelts is that they are not big enough. Most are only between two and ten miles wide. No development is permitted within the greenbelt, so you have a city inside it. Yet on the outer edge, development begins again. If these greenbelts interlocked with urbanized wilderness corridors, which lead to city parks and other open areas inside urbanized spaces, the combination of the greenbelts, corridors, and parks could function like an ecological replica of what would naturally be there. They could be connected to existing natural trails, greenways, and other recreational spaces through a system of linear structures that act as bridges and stopgaps, overpasses, and underpasses.

Oddly enough, there are examples of such eco-bridges and pathways, although not yet in the context of cities. To help mitigate the problem of large animals turning into roadkill, sustainable highway design has begun bridging over freeways and interstates in many countries. The designs are simple overpasses or underpasses located at important wildlife corridors. Different sites will determine where such crossings occur. Typically, if, say, spawning areas are directly on the other side, a crossing would best be placed at that point. Other determining factors can be a change in elevation that would be a natural place for easy access. Water and food sources also determine where animals typically travel. These structures are designed to look to the animals like natural landscape with trees, grass, brush, and other aspects of the surroundings. Sustainable highways have proven ideal for creating safe pathways for animals. In the early 1990s, Florida panthers were in danger of becoming extinct because of deaths related to collisions with cars. The techniques of sustainable highway design were used to reduce roadkill deaths of the big cats. After they were constructed throughout the state, fatalities began to decrease in number, and the Florida panther population stabilized. These innovative transportation designs have been used in Europe and Canada to protect both wildlife and motorists.

Research has found that two major factors determine the success or failure of such efforts: one, that an ecological perspective is better than focusing on an individual species; and two, that compatible land use needs to be an integral part to how wildlife passages are incorporated into highway structures.[8] The ecological perspective looks at the situation and asks where the most important and richest lands can be found, and what can be done to enhance the full spectrum of the ecosystem. A focus on one species would ask questions like, what is the best habitat for this individual animal? The answer disregards the greater biology. Wildlife crossings have been found to work best when built to be asymmetrical instead of symmetrical. Humans want to see things as regular and even. As noted, in nature, things do not always work out like that.[9] In combination with asymmetrical crossings, compactable land use is another protocol for wildlife crossings, meaning that the crossing structure seamlessly fits into the terrain and that patterns of rock, grass, trees, and other natural features are maintained. You want to make sure that both sides are safe and nothing on either side would frighten animals from the area.[10]

The structures themselves are less defined—no single solution fits all. In general, the highway accessory should be a product of the surrounding environment. For example, outside of Wismar, Germany, a green bridge was constructed as an overpass for the autobahn to protect mammals, birds, and other species.[11] Green bridges are used in the western half of the United States to allow connectivity for grizzly bears and other large animals. Other options such as multiuse structures (which double as pedestrian and bicycle bridges and include a lane covered with vegetation and natural features for wildlife crossing), noise barriers (which provide nesting areas for birds), fencing (which guides wildlife to crossing areas), and underpasses (which serve dual functions of facilitating drainage patterns and wildlife movements) are other ways to help members of a variety of species reconnect when highway construction causes fragmentation.[12] Simple structures such as tunnels and large pipes can be utilized when small animals such as salamanders and turtles are targeted for reconnectivity efforts. For years after the first spring rains in Amherst, Massachusetts, volunteers shuttled buckets of spotted salamanders across Henry Street in the middle of town to prevent them from being killed under the tires of traffic. Two-lane Henry Street separates salamanders from the warm, fishless vernal pools (small temporary ponds) where they migrate every spring to mate and to lay their eggs. Then in 1987, the shuttling volunteers' work was done after two tunnels, 200 feet apart, were built at the exact location necessary for the salamanders to cross to the other side. A short drift fence that guides them toward the tunnel was also built. A salamander "xing" sign marks the spot.[13]

Taking these proven methods of greening transportation and applying them to the green roofs of the future is a natural next step. Without such improvements, green roofs will not be any better for connecting ecosystems than well-manicured lawns. If green roofs become interlocked with park spaces, and wildlife corridors are formed throughout urbanized areas, they can influence the future development of homes and commercial buildings. Ecological principles defined by conservation biologists could help in the development of guidelines for how suburban sprawl should be redesigned as well as identify where densification of suburbs should and should not occur and redefine what wilderness and civilization are.

Wilderness as a feature for urban areas has huge benefits for people. Unless big steps are taken, vast, untamed woodlands will disappear. So many people have never really seen a vast landscape of undisturbed wilderness. We are more used to seeing nature as a park or maybe a rural area that is dotted with houses and roads. Wild places do exist, but only in faraway places like in the northern Canadian and Russian boreal forests, in the tundra of Greenland, in the Amazon basin, in parts of Africa like the Serengeti, in the mountain ranges of Eastern Europe, and in the arid deserts scattered on different continents. Large wildernesses—more than 50 percent of all designated wilderness in the United States—are still present in Alaska. The remainder are in the lower 48 states in such places as Raggeds Wilderness, located northwest of Crested Butte, Colorado; Red Rock Lakes Wilderness, in southwest Montana; and Yosemite National Park in east-central California. In 2003, Russell Mittermeier, president of Conservation International, published a book entitled *Wilderness: Earth's Last Wild Places.* Based on the criteria that the book outlined for what a wilderness is (in terms of size, intactness, human density, and biodiversity), only 37 areas were identified. A total of eight were partly in the United States, including the Mojave Desert, the Appalachians, and the Colorado Plateau.[14]

In such places, the human world is absent, and the ecological services operate with complete precision. For example, old-growth forests remove carbon dioxide from the atmosphere. The sequestered CO_2 is stored in woody tissues, the leaves, and soil. Old-growth forests are a primary ecological feature of mature temperate and boreal forests. Old-growth forests are only one type of carbon sink within nature. Estuaries and watersheds have also been shown to have a significant ability to capture CO_2 at a faster rate than other natural lands.

Other ecosystems are hard at work moderating weather extremes and their impacts, dispersing seeds, mitigating drought and floods, cycling and moving nutrients, protecting stream and river channels and coastal shores from erosion, detoxifying and decomposing wastes, controlling agricultural pests, maintaining biodiversity, generating and preserving soils, and renewing their fertility—just to name a few. If we expect our planet to continue to provide us with these services in the years and decades to come, we will have to take real steps toward preserving, and restoring, them soon.

Fortunately, restoring habitat on a grand scale is already under way, and many large-scale ecological programs have been suggested throughout the

United States. One is the Algonquin to Adirondack Connectivity Zone, which would connect Algonquin Provincial Park, in Ontario, Canada, to the Adirondack Park in New York State by an uninterrupted wilderness corridor. Another large-scale connectivity project is a 70,000 square mile area in the Sky Islands region of southeastern Arizona, southwestern New Mexico, and northwestern Mexico. It sits at the southern tip of the Rocky Mountains and between the Sonoran and Chihuahuan Deserts. Forested ranges are separated by vast expanses of desert and grassland plains. They are among the most diverse ecosystems in the world because of their great topographic complexity and unique location at the meeting point of several major desert and forest biological provinces. The biodiversity encompasses over half the bird species of North America, 29 bat species, over 3,000 species of plants, and 104 species of mammals, including the Mexican wolf, jaguar, and wild ocelot. If any or all of these projects were undertaken and completed, similar numbers of species and relative amounts of land would be conserved comparable to the number saved after the wolves were reintroduced to Yellowstone National Park.

Yet all of these projects are in lightly populated areas. The closest major cities to Yellowstone National Park are Salt Lake City, Utah, and Denver, Colorado—both more than 250 miles away and both with less than a million people in the core city (the metropolitan areas of Denver and Salt Lake City have more than a million people). Though Adirondack Park is in the same state as New York City, the park is more than five hours away by car and has an average population density of 42 people per square mile in the surrounding counties. It's not adequate to only improve lands far away from more densely populated areas. Though the concentration of people will be throughout megalopolises in the coming years, the amount of land already modified by human activity has left little to be reverted to large, free wilderness. Also, the ideal of us being in one place and nature being in a different place maintains the idea that we are not all of nature. The dynamic of urban centers dictates more tremendous natural intrusion than is obvious at first. Urbanites are as dependent on the extraction of agriculture and mining products as those in rural areas. Also, ecological services need to be present throughout core cities and rural areas. We need watersheds providing clean water in Detroit, Michigan, as much as we need them in Austin, Texas, and San Diego, California. The urbanization of land in countries around the world is a global trend. Bringing wilderness home is essential to show examples that can be exported to other countries and continents.

Without the reestablishment of such areas, long-term solutions will be difficult, if not impossible to solve. Carbon emissions are usually talked about from the perspective that we need to reduce fossil fuel consumption or change from one fuel to a different fuel to decrease carbon in the atmosphere. Others call for technology-based solutions to sequester carbon. These are all misguided solutions. Billions of dollars are wasted every year trying to solve these issues with high-tech answers, when a fraction of that funding directed toward conservation and reforesting could remedy them once and for all.

In the coming decades, we need to begin to create a framework that aims to preserve and protect the functionality of our ecosystems on an unprecedented scale. We will have to rethink and redesign old concepts about infrastructure and delivery systems as well as integrate biology expertise into new buildings, while retrofitting older ones in this new, and greener, model.

The combined result of wildlife corridors from coastal areas to the inland, oyster reef restoration to improve water quality, and the protection of watersheds would improve the life of people in ways that technology could not do. For one, it would bring the human world and the natural world much closer together, and allow us to design cities, metropolises, and megalopolises from the point of view that we are one with nature already.

It is not that we can have either ecology or technology—that is the wrong attitude. The dream of a renatured world should be a desire for all that believe in the future of humanity—rewilded lands will provide life, giving support to all living things. Emerging technologies in green building allow planners and ecologists to envision more flexible infrastructure and to use it to help direct development into more ecologically sound patterns.

Green building has found its way into the curriculum of many architectural and engineering departments at universities around the globe. At least, the kind of green building talked about in the early chapters of this book. Conservation biology is not taught to students studying architecture. This is a serious problem, as megalopolises continue to grow, and the call for projects like smart grids and utility scale renewable energy projects becomes louder.

It is hard to predict exactly how green building will mature. Examples of green building today and where it is likely to be tomorrow are laying the groundwork for creating amazing opportunities with economic growth as well as fundamental changes within urban design that could foster wilderness in close proximity to cities and beyond. Can we be as beneficial as a beaver, or an oyster? It seems odd that the challenge is not in being the smartest, fastest, most powerful living organism—the challenge is learning to be the most helpful. We can have every building in the world become more energy efficient. We can create mega-installations of solar power and wind turbines that blanket the Mojave Desert and the Great Plains, as well as line the East and West Coasts. We can install a supersmart grid that regulates energy from Maine to Nevada, and we can build huge waterworks that take water from the Great Lakes so people in Arizona can keep their lawns green. If this were to happen, some would see it as an awesome victory, but in truth it would exacerbate a whole host of problems from water purity and supply to the need to maintain an expensive and unwieldy electrical grid. And it would further intrude on the natural environment, making it increasingly difficult for diverse ecosystems around the world to provide us with the ecological services that we are accustomed to. For everyone and all other species, it would be a far cry from a more perfect union between nature and civilization. The architecture of tomorrow cannot be only a monument to human ingenuity; it must also be a powerful example of nature's preexisting wonder. Our challenge for the future is to embrace ecological sustainability as the first and best solution. But for now, we are still the anti-keystone species.

CHAPTER 10

THE INVISIBLE CITY

What could society look like in a century? That depends on the decisions we make today and tomorrow. Some trends show that we are moving in the direction of clean energy versus renewable energy, and where we are moving toward renewable energy, it is toward utility scale renewable energy versus micro-infrastructure renewable energy. Even within the green building community, it seems we are more interested in technology than in ecology, and in saving energy more than in saving nature. In this last section, I will present what it would look like if a shift from big, inflexible, technological-based architecture to a small, natural, highly adaptable architecture were to happen. This is a critical side to the future of architecture in being more aligned with conservation biology and sustainability in general. If we continue to build as we do today, no room will be left for ecological services to offset the impact society has. Likewise, megalopolises will need a disproportionate amount of water and energy than other areas throughout the country. Identifying inexpensive solutions for networks and systems such as the energy grid and waterworks is the only way we may be able to afford our future demand.

The shift of populations from one geographical locale to another, most often from rural and former manufacturing communities to cosmopolitan centers, is in lockstep with the growth of megalopolises, and it's changing the way many think about buildings. This demographic transition will make it easier to build a future for our country where ecomimicry is implemented at a large scale, along with regrowing old-growth forests and preserving ecosystems, for the betterment of water quality, human health, and species diversity.

ECOMIMICRY AND THE FUTURE OF CITIES

It is important to note that architecture, as well as engineering, design, and construction, are client-based professions. They do not do anything that is not okayed by who is paying them for their services. This is an awkward position, but they also could become more involved in the crafting of projects at all levels from policy for governmental agencies to working with real estate developers. Such a move could transform the practice of green from a reactionary mentality to a solution-oriented mindset. Those who champion plug-in electric cars are as driven by the reaction of being against petroleum from the Middle East as they are for carbon reduction. The goal of utility scale renewable energy is reacting to pollution caused by fossil fuels—but does not think through the reasons why so much energy is needed in the first place. Even proponents of green buildings are currently trying to figure out how to minimize environmental impact instead of restoring ecology or eliminating the need for energy altogether. Currently, the business of design and construction isn't making room for hydrologists and ecologists, yet they bring the creativity and amazing insight to solving problems that are needed for green projects.

Ecomimicry interlocks the human world with wilderness—making them mutually beneficial. It is the practice of applying design, science, and engineering to restore or improve ecological services and, in some cases, function as a proxy for ecosystems. It's not limited to any one scale of project such as a structure or city—in fact, to work completely, ecomimicry needs to be applied to everything that we build, from small projects like buildings or subdivisions to the scale of a region, nation, and transnational agglomerate. It's vital to understand that ecomimicry doesn't simply call for designs to imitate natural processes, but that ecosystems should be the foundation of the design. Ecomimicry is the actual ecosystematic function graphed upon civilization.

Humans are a major driver of ecosystems already. When we are introduced into a habitat, we typically degrade it by building things, as we always have. However, it is not just animals such as ourselves that can dramatically impact the environment. Some trees are keystone species. They have a lot less biomass than all the other species and soils present in nature, but they manage to dictate a number of factors, from hydrology to temperature as well as habitat conditions and food opportunities. Humans are presently doing the same thing, except that trees typically increase biodiversity while humans are decreasing it. Our influence, for better or worse, is setting the course many species are taking. Unfortunately, the course they are taking is toward extinction.

The change from a conventional means of building to an ecomimicry approach can be illustrated by imagining the effort necessary to redesign and retrofit a swath of land from the Grand Canyon to Mexico City. Currently, there are both highly urbanized, domesticated lands along with less populated terrain. Such an eco-region would run through Phoenix, Santa Fe, and Denver, down through several fragile ecosystems like the Chihuahuan Desert. How do you create highways and other transportation systems that encourage biodiversity? Where will water come from, and how can it be shared with other species? How do you organize cities and economic centers to generate jobs, energy, profits, and homes for millions of people, while establishing niches for a wide array of native animals and plants? For such a change in design to happen, a new vision for land use will need to be backed by policy. Architects and civil engineers will need to be highly versed in ecological sciences and biology. Water and energy budgeting will have to outsmart old ways of determining where buildings are and are not built. We will have to be smarter about how we preserve wilderness so as to preserve ecological services. And we will have to accept we are part of nature, not apart from it.

The end goal would be to have this revitalized region support a population of tens of millions of people while producing the natural niches for multiple ecosystems of native plants and animals to flourish and abound, where agriculture, infrastructure, and power production is integrated into nature in a way that enriches rivers, forests, economics, and communities. Such a project would be massively complex, and would need a multinational/interstate effort and a tremendous amount of professional know-how and dedication. Biologists, engineers, ecologists, architects, zoologists, designers, hydrologists, and a host of other disciplines would need to work together to restore multiple eco-zones along with reintroducing and fostering populations of species throughout the landscape, and restoring geological and ecological features artificially removed by man.

Through a vast network of human-to-nature connections, grounded in ecomimicry, a more symbiotic, beneficial relationship would emerge. Ecosystems do lots of valuable things for humans that we seldom know. Trees help filter particulates out of the air, making it less damaging to our respiratory system. They also stabilize soil with their root systems and regulate the speed of growth for other plants under their canopies. In turn, the moisture contained in the earth helps keep temperatures stable and encourages more predictable rainfall. Healthy dirt along with strong plant communities filter water as it moves toward creeks, rivers, lakes, and estuaries. The result is better quality of rudimentary components for human life. There is a potentially huge economic benefit too, such as New York City saving billions of dollars each year in filtration costs because of the healthiness of the reservoirs and watersheds that supply its water. Ecomimicry calls for the integration of human civilization with the components of the natural world essential for ecological health so that all species have the ability to thrive, not just survive.

Currently, these are concerns chiefly dealt with by ecologists and biologists, but these issues are largely absent from the curriculum and training of architects and engineers. It is not just the problem of design schools. Biologists and ecologists are not educated about urban design, infrastructure, or construction. To help designers better understand what's vital for ecology, they must first learn the science behind the fundamental factors making up all of the complexity for the development of life on Earth.

This is the perfect moment for architects and designers to embrace this subject matter because our understanding of the biological working of this planet is only beginning to be appreciated by the general public. Just as green building has sparked numerous businesses, new products, and a new awareness of building better—ecomimicry would do the same, only this time at a much larger scale. Worldwide, a few professionals (designers or scientists) are working on reintroducing ecological functionality to society. If ecomimicry is instituted as the way of tackling things from real estate development to infrastructure design, new wealth and a new age of discovery would eclipse anything currently in the market. In Singapore, the government is working to align its water usage with the natural patterns of rainfall and watersheds. They are treating wastewater so well that it has become potable again, and you can buy it bottled. They have turned parts of the country into water catchment areas to fill reservoirs full of storm water. These efforts are allowing them to supply 60 percent of their own needs, and in 50 years, they hope to be 100 percent self-sufficient.[1] In the United States, projects such as those at Withers Swash and Wilson Bay are examples of how designers and biologists are rethinking watershed protection with urban design. In order to be truly revolutionary, these types of projects need to stretch for hundreds of miles, where currently they are small and localized. Conservation biology and green building can reinforce each other and make each other smarter, more relevant, and more apt to enrich all life for the better.

Researchers, ecologists, conservationists, and scientists are finding that three ecosystems have a wide variety of carbon sequestering properties: prairies, estuaries, and old-growth forests. As you will see, the pattern of depopulation in the Great Plains is making for real opportunities to establish vast wildernesses within the United States. Also, in places like eastern Germany, the same opportunities are being presented. These three areas should be seen as the framework to set forth plans for urban areas and infrastructure. The common notion that cities are places absent of nature could be replaced with ecologically based efforts to restore such habitats. If coastal metropolises restored estuaries to their original sizes, large portions would be completely natural. These areas would serve as park space as well as a real-world answer to climate change. Moreover, innovations would be necessary to monitor the health of the habitats along with caretakers trained in urban design, ecology, and climate science. Technologies to measure the rate of carbon capture would need to be invented and designed for deployment in dozens of areas around the world. Along with these benefits, air quality would be improved with large native lands at the edges of megacities along with many other ecological services. Current efforts to build green cities are not thinking along these lines. They are solely focused on technological sustainability, overlooking the economic and social advantages of more natural options.

FUTURE CITIES TODAY

The green buildings of today are beginning to foster futuristic cities around the world. With the growth of economic powers like China along with global hotspots like Dubai, many leaders and designers have joined forces to win the race as the first green city to showcase how they see the future unfolding.

In 2005, Dongtan, a project on the island of Chongming outside of Shanghai, China, was hailed as the "first eco-city." At completion, it would have been a development the size of Manhattan with a cultural and urban richness to match. The masterminds behind the project were the famous British engineering company ARUP, in partnership with Chinese developers and officials. Dignitaries, such as former British Prime Minister Tony Blair, were present at the signing of the contract for the project. The project was to deal directly with common problems in cities like human and environmental health, energy, economic vitality and individual prosperity, mobility and access, water, and materials and waste, along with governance and civic engagement. Some of the key principles of their sustainable framework included preserving the area's natural habitats and carbon neutrality.

The team planned for a compact city situated on the far side of a wetlands preserve. Instead of bulldozing the wetlands and building on top, the designers saw that by saving them they could act as a buffer between the city and the Yangtze River Delta. The design would reduce the ecological footprint of each citizen by as much as 70 percent.

When the eco-city was first announced, it was received by the world media, green designers, political leaders, and the like with great excitement. Only in a country growing as fast and building as feverishly as China could such a design, incorporating the newest green technologies, be proposed and executed. The first phase of the project was to be completed by 2010—but by 2007 and 2008 no construction had started except a bridge to connect the island to Shanghai. The worst was assumed and then verified. The project was "dead in the water."[2] Reports suggest that confusion about who was supposed to fund the project was the death-strike to the Donghan green giant. This is not uncommon in the construction world. There are more projects designed every year than are actually built. Even the projects with the greatest promise often never make it to fruition. Nevertheless, the attempt to incorporate all of these goals into a massive urban planning project is a good sign. Many lessons can be learned from Donghan. One is that scientists, developers, and designers can work together to create a hybrid between pure urban area and natural lands. The project was stopped not because the combination of green and ecology does not work, but because of bad financial planning. It is essential that financial professionals understand how the two will increase the short- and long-term benefits of projects. Governments will prove themselves very smart when water sources are more available due to watershed protection and they do not need to spend money on filtration as the cities mature. Experienced designers and teams need to be involved with large city-scale projects from the beginning. Anyone who has been in the green building industry for years knows that green buildings are unique cases that need innovative economic models to prove out investment.

Huangbaiyu, located in northern China in an area traditionally home to thousands of farmers and laborers, is another example of an eco-city that failed to come to fruition. This time it was proposed by William McDonough, one of the founding architects of the green building movement. The project planned to revamp an existing village, turning it into a state-of-the-art city. Original graphics were created for a compact city with rooftop agriculture on every building. The homes were to be constructed of local materials like hay and rammed earth to keep prices affordable for the low-income residents. When the first 42 houses were completed, they averaged about $24,000. By American standards they were cheap; however, for the locals that was about six times more expensive than they could afford. Not only that, but the local residents did not find the homes livable. The houses did not face south—a mistake for both solar orientation and cultural spiritual relevance. In a location where nearly everyone is mobile only by foot, some of the houses had garages. Plus, the homes were located too far away from their fields and other work places, causing too much time wasted in commuting. Critics have said that the development is too American for the people of China. The rows of houses are built as if they are in a suburb in Florida instead of a village. Huangbaiyu failed because McDonough never interfaced with the community to understand what they needed or wanted in the retrofitting of their village. Community involvement has hitherto not been a regular component for many real estate developers. The relationship between citizen and developer is often adversarial—and for good reason. Famous examples include Robert Moses reimagining lower Manhattan as an interstate interchange—which Jane Jacobs famously blocked through grassroots organization. On the one hand, many people within a community are cautious about change; but on the other, urban renewal can bring about needed jobs and commerce. Pitfalls are always present, from the destruction of the community fabric to the financial failure of speculative projects. Many of the failures come from breaking one fundamental rule about design—the buildings need to fit the client. Clients are the source of what is constructed, or more simply, you do not design a birdcage for a dog. Nor do you design a doghouse for a bird. Green design takes the concept one step further. Designs need to fit into the local climate and surroundings. In the case of Huangbaiyu, houses were not ideal for the cold winters. This would have made them costly to heat from November to March when temperatures can drop to 10 degrees or less. Every green city should strongly consider weather patterns before even starting the design process. A full and exhaustive climatic analysis would inform a project so as to save money on energy from the very start. A home designed on weather data can save up to 25 percent on energy. Plus, all homes need to be right-sized, meaning that if you are designing for villages, residents may not need or want 5,000 square feet. That is essential to know from the beginning as well.

Other examples exist as roadmaps for greener cities. Not all attempts to build an eco-city in China have failed. The Sino-Singapore Tianjin Eco-city, east of Beijing, is showing that it learned from the problems of its predecessors. Today the race is on to build the first eco-city worldwide. Masdar City, in Abu Dhabi, is aiming to be the first-built carbon neutral city. The city, measuring 2.3 square miles, broke ground in early 2008 and is scheduled to be completed by 2050. The city is designed by the British architectural firm Foster + Partners, and will be home to more than 50,000 people and 1,500 businesses.

Upon completion, Masdar City will be reliant solely on solar energy and other renewable energy sources. Features include a 60 megawatt solar power plant and a 20 megawatt wind farm, while residential units in the development are designed to use 54 percent less water and 51 percent less electricity than average residences in the United Arab Emirates. The city occupants hope to get 30 percent of the buildings' electricity needs from solar panels installed on rooftops and 75 percent of their hot water from rooftop thermal collectors. Other innovations like geothermal energy and solar thermal cooling are being explored as potential sources of power.

Of course this brings into question whether we should be building cities in the middle of a desert. The desert is a good place to generate native energy from solar panels, and could probably support a large city with on-site energy. But to say the development is using 54 percent less water is misleading. The average rainfall in the area is a mere three and half inches a year—that is less rain than Las Vegas receives annually. Five months of the year, there is no precipitation at all on average. Local sources of water can't support such a city as Masdar City—so the water that the city does need will be either piped in from far away or created from desalination plants, which take extreme amounts of energy to run. This is why practices like water budgeting are necessary. To call a city green that is completely out of step with the local environment sends a message that anything can be called green as long as green gadgets and gizmos are applied to the design. Green has to be more in tune with the hydrological and energy realities of the area. Simply building massive new cities in places that can't support the populations is, in essence, creating a future environmental problem. At some point such a city will overtax the surrounding area of food, energy, water, or another necessity. Moreover, if the economic strength of Abu Dhabi ever shrinks or the costs of infrastructure become too high, the municipalities will have trouble maintaining healthy and safe conditions for the people living in Masdar City.

In many ways, Donghan, Huangbaiyu, and Masdar City are no different from all the other cities before them. They do show the direction today's leading architects and city planners are taking in turning the current ideas of green building into a reality. They choose to embrace technological sustainability, while doing little to incorporate water budgeting or ecology, and are not even approaching the ideal of ecomimicry. In fact, in 2010, developers of Masdar City released plans to no longer produce all of the city's own clean energy on-site, but to purchase energy from other regions.[3] But perhaps more than anything, these eco-cities are trying to confront the fact that the earth's population is continuing to grow.

HOW SHIFTING DEMOGRAPHICS CREATE NEW OPPORTUNITIES FOR ECOMIMICRY

With a projected 9 billion people on the planet by 2050, and a projected 75 percent of them in cities, it would seem a little crazy if people were not thinking about how to deal with more and more people in smaller and smaller spaces. Currently there are 40 or so megalopolises scattered around the planet, with an estimated 3.5 billion people living in these urban areas. In the United States, 80 percent of people, or just under 250 million, live in megalopolises. Even more will move to these areas in the coming years. The growth will test our ability to accommodate

the additional population of our cities, stressing water supply, energy efficiency, transportation effectiveness, economic stability, and habitat restoration. In fact, we are already seeing many of these approaching the
breaking point. Today's green building practices are a last-ditch effort to
avoid complete meltdown.

With current projections of growth, major cities, urban areas, and
megalopolises are likely to take up less than 10 percent of the land area in
the United States. That leaves a huge chunk as rural. Some of that land
is devoted to farms, pastures, and ranges, but many are closing. Families
and farmers are giving up on the hard life in places like North Dakota,
Kansas, and Iowa to migrate to cities in search of jobs and better lifestyles.[4] Surprisingly, this could be a pathway to the ecological integration
of wilderness and urbanization.

While the population in the rest of the world booms, places like northern Japan, Russia, Italy, and Middle America are emptying due to a mix of
reasons: industries being outsourced, low birthrates, migration to urban
areas as well as cultural and generational shifts toward careers. Of all the
places facing decline, Europe will change the most. In 1963, Europeans
living in Europe represented nearly 13 percent of the world's populace;
today, that number has almost been cut in half, and by 2050, Europeans
will represent only 5 percent of the people on the planet. North America,
thanks to a healthy birthrate and immigration, is not in any danger of
shrinking as a whole. But the core cities of the United States are. This is
why it is important to understand the growth patterns of megalopolises.
Core cities are just a part of them, not the reason they exist. In the Boston
to Washington mega-region, the major core cities like New York, Boston,
and Washington have done well to maintain and grow in population over
the last 40 years. In other regions that is not true.

The Great Lakes megalopolis, made up of Chicago, Toronto, Detroit,
Cleveland, Pittsburgh, and Buffalo, is the embodiment of how cities can
fall. Of the cities making up the megalopolis, Detroit, Cleveland, Buffalo,
and Pittsburgh have all experienced loss in population of 45 percent or
more. Detroit has lost more than a million residents since 1950, making

it one of the most vacated places in the country, second only to New Orleans, which has seen a mass exodus since Hurricane Katrina. However, their metropolitan areas have not lost population at the same rate. Their suburbs have seen more jobs created, better economic growth, and higher populations even as the core cities have shrunk. One major reason is that living in a core city is usually more expensive than living in a subdivision just outside of it. Second, as enough people begin to live on the outskirts, a suburb can begin to support economic growth without the core city to which it is adjacent, so then there is no reason for living or working in the major city. This is attractive for those unemployed in rural areas looking for work. If they move into either a suburb (which is more affordable) or a core city (which is less affordable), their chances of finding employment increase dramatically. Both the suburban communities and core cities are considered urbanized. It is this combination of city and suburb that is home to 80 percent of all Americans. This relationship will only intensify during the next few decades with other metropolitan areas slowly overlapping to form megalopolises.

Towns like Northville, Farmington Hills, and Ann Arbor are all within the metropolitan area of Detroit and are thriving while Detroit itself is not. The core city has fewer people than it did in 1920, but overall, the metropolitan area has grown. If new life is breathed into industries throughout Michigan, more jobs will likely spring up, but Detroit may not see any improvements. Massive exoduses can cause a great many problems for those people who remain in the cities as well as the governments in charge of maintaining them. For one, urban design is based on growth in our society. In fact, all of the planning and decision-making about core cities, towns, suburbs, and metropolitan areas are always based on growth. Yet, as places like Detroit lose people, four major problems begin to appear.[5] The first is that with fewer people within the city limits, local governments lose tax revenue and have less money to maintain the city. Second, younger and more educated residents are the most likely to leave, causing economic and cultural stagnation within the urban area. These two symptoms combine to generate a third major problem: a loss in quality of life for those still in the city. The collapse of lifestyle also discourages others from moving into the area—exacerbating the problem of decreased tax revenue even more. The final problem, and the most difficult to manage, is that too much public infrastructure is left to maintain. These municipal systems were designed to service much larger populations—but as urban decay results in fewer people, they cannot function correctly even if they could be maintained. This quickly creates a vicious cycle downward.

The cycle started as companies moved their operations from the United States to other countries at the same time as telecommunications advances allowed factories and management to be in different locations. Historically, cities were the center of industrial power, but that has completely changed today. Today, urban centers depend on an influx of people, businesses, and tourism to stay alive. The goal is to reap the benefits for the upward motion of expansion. This is the mentality that determined how infrastructure was built in the United States. During low points in the economy, when labor and materials were cheapest, dams, bridges, waterworks, and energy systems were built. Over time, this approach has given us infrastructure that is too expensive to maintain and too expensive to replace. Looking into the future, we should recognize that growth is not always the direction for every city and town. More flexibility should be built into our systems so as to be able to respond to changes in either direction. The eco-cities of the world are thinking only in terms of growth, not shrinkage. From the examples in China and Abu Dhabi and with cities like New York and Mexico City developing green planning practices, officials are doing so because all projections point toward explosive growth during the next century. New York City has developed the GreeNYC to meet sustainability goals for a growing populace, but it is the exception, not the rule. Suburban sprawl and the outlying areas of core cities will see the greatest growth in the next few decades, not the core cities. The difference between the demographics of New York and Detroit highlights that cities and megalopolises are either growing or shrinking. The urbanscape of America, and globally, shows that some places are growing and some are not, but in both cases, the cities were designed with the idea that they would always be growing. The Northeast megalopolis is winning the competition of jobs and economic growth. The Great Lake megacities may not recover. If jobs begin to dry up, people will leave looking for work in other regions of the country.

Where there are no core cities or suburban sprawl, people are leaving for good. No other place in the world has seen this like the Great Plains in the middle of America. From North Dakota to west Texas, there is a lack of bustling metropolitan areas, save Kansas City, Des Moines, and Oklahoma City—all of which have fewer than 600,000 people. Without the foundation of major cities, people are moving farther away in search of jobs. With the decline of the cities and suburbs, rural areas are also emptying out. Many of the counties throughout the Great Plains have fewer people in them than were there a century ago.

The problem is so bad that many cities appear to be dying. New Orleans and Detroit are the largest cities in danger of this. Other, lesser known cities like Canton, Youngstown, and Dayton, Ohio, and Flint, Michigan, are suffering from high unemployment, economic troubles, and serious population loss. All of these places were once thriving semi- to true cosmopolitan cities, with the big, bulky infrastructure that comes with that.

Of the dying cities, one rising star is Youngstown, Ohio. Situated halfway between New York and Chicago, it was once a boomtown. From 1820 to 1870, the town saw nearly 200 percent growth, and by 1930 had more than 170,000 residents. The past few years have not been as kind. Since then, the town has lost nearly 100,000 people with no real end in sight. With more than 4,500 vacant structures and a declining tax base from an ever-shrinking population, it is facing critical issues. If you walked down its streets today, you would see maybe one manicured lawn for every five to ten blocks of abandoned and boarded-up housing. Facing thousands of empty lots, or worse, structures in such disrepair that they were endangering the remaining populace, the leadership of the city decided to embrace their new status as a shrinking city.

In 2005, a city-wide plan was adopted entitled Youngstown 2010. Its main goal was to "right-size" the town to fit its realities while, at the same time, improving Youngstown's image and enhancing quality of life. Starting in 2006, city officials began demolishing structures to improve property values and reduce pressure to infrastructure. The city demolished 351 in the first year, then in 2007 another 474, and in 2008 another 103. The plan created incentives for people to relocate from one part of the town to another to curb the need for the expansive piping and electrical grid. Since keeping roads is expensive, city officials tried to figure out which streets could be closed. They found that this was harder than they thought. Closing one road could hinder emergency vehicles like fire trucks and ambulances from gaining fast access to homes and other areas during emergencies. But progress was being made.

As dilapidated buildings were removed, open parcels replaced them, creating new green spaces and the potential for city gardens and parks. Organizations have sprung up like Grow Youngstown, which advocates for urban agriculture and distributes fresh, local produce to underserved neighborhoods in the city. The Youngstown Neighborhood Development Corporation is working to turn blocks of blight into long urban gardens as well as bring innovative approaches for business development. Youngstown State University is working with the city to establish a wetlands mitigation bank, and thereby improve the ecological value of the area with more biodiversity. The wetlands also help to reduce the cost of maintaining land, because they are self-sustaining.

These efforts have not completely stopped the dwindling of the population, nor have they changed the course of its economy, at least not yet. City officials did not have any precedent for their decision to embrace getting smaller, but they knew if they did not include the public from the beginning, their efforts would not be successful. They formed public committees and a partnership with the citizens. With the first round complete, the work has brought about some positive changes.

The Youngstown Business Incubator, which started in 1998 with financial support from the State of Ohio, mentors new companies with networking and services like office space and bandwidth for free or at a deferred cost. One success story from the incubator is Turning Technologies, which grossed $33.5 million in 2009. That same year, *Entrepreneur* magazine listed Youngstown as one of the ten places in America "Where to Be an Entrepreneur."[6] These types of successes are good for Youngstown—and are helping places as far away as Japan and as near as Detroit see one perspective on how to deal with a shrinking city. But people are still leaving Youngstown, and those who left have not yet come back. Photographer Greg Miller described Youngstown as having "apocalyptic emptiness" during his narration for a photojournalistic piece for *Inc.* magazine even after all the revival.[7] In the end, most of the shrinking and dying cities throughout the world will stay empty—the beautification via gardens and parks will help those who stay, but a strategy to embrace decrease will probably create more decrease. The surrounding areas may very well become more populated—the feeling of an apocalyptic event is not usually what people are looking for in a new home or school district. Growth rates in towns around core cities are typically faster. The once mighty metropolises will be the donut holes within mega-regions. This will only solidify the already-established pattern of megalopolises.

Where there are no megalopolises, major cities, or metropolitan areas, you'll find entire states and regions emptying. Depopulation is causing the same problems throughout the 500,000 square miles of the Great Plains that it is causing in Youngstown and Detroit. Infrastructure costs are exceeding tax revenues. When the Ogallala Aquifer is no longer available for irrigation, the farmers in the region will have only two choices: abandon their farms or pay for and construct massive waterworks to deliver water to them. And with cities in Colorado, Nevada, California, and Arizona sucking the Colorado River dry, the only option would be the Great Lakes. The ramifications of using the Great Lakes as the source of water for the Southwest would devastate the environment and hurt the economy of the states surrounding them. The usage of the lakes as a way to ship imports and exports could easily be hampered. Their aquatic habitats are already under pressure from existing demands. Many fish are already endangered, including the lake sturgeon. The sturgeons are considered a living fossil because they have remained almost unchanged for the last 65 million years.

Lake sturgeons were abundant until the nineteenth century, when the lakes became increasingly populated.[8]

Climate change is predicted to dramatically alter the Great Lakes region by making the large bodies of freshwater shallower and dirtier. That means less water for the people already depending on it. Places such as Buffalo will face higher water costs and lower water quality. Tourism at the beaches could be affected by closures from the increased amounts of pollutants. The falling lake levels will eliminate access to some docks, harbors, and marinas.[9] Kansas is one place where the emptying was detected as far back as the 1980s by Frank and Deborah Popper.[10] They predicted that depopulation would stress local economies, infrastructure, and culture, and that preemptive measures could be taken to ensure long-term benefits. The Poppers suggested most of the prairies be returned to native lands, and allow buffalo, pronghorn, and other endemic species to roam entirely free of obstacles—sort of a multistate, 100,000 square mile national park. At the time the paper was first published, residents revolted against the idea, criticizing it as a rebuke to their way of life and claiming that the Poppers were out-of-touch, out-of-town academics. The idea was also offensive to then-Kansas governor Mike Hayden, who thought that the projections of massive depopulation of the Great Plains were simply "city logic," and didn't believe that it could happen.[11]

Today if you look at Kansas as a whole, the population has increased but only slightly, with the majority of the state's population now living in the northeastern areas of the state in counties like Johnson and Leavenworth—both within the metropolitan area of Kansas City, Missouri (population: 2,053,000). Of the 105 counties, only 25 have seen positive population growth since the 1980s. All others have depopulated, and now Kansas has nearly 6,000 ghost towns.[12] In 2004, Hayden admitted during a speech at Kansas State University that he was wrong about disbelieving the Poppers.[13] In fact, after 20 years of witnessing the lack of development in Kansas, he said the Poppers were too conservative on what they thought about the future. Today, many in Kansas are fighting to create a national park in the spirit of the Poppers' report. The benefits could include increased ecotourism dollars, as grasslands are the world's most endangered ecosystem and reestablishing a large patch is important to America's natural and cultural heritage. The prairie is also the greatest long-term carbon sequestration landscape available, as the grasses take carbon from the atmosphere and bury it deep in the ground, where it stays to nurture plant growth.

Today, the Great Plains remain extremely endangered. Less than 1 percent of the American prairie, originally covering from North Dakota to Texas and Indiana to Wyoming, remains. From the standpoint of eco-mimicry, letting the Great Plains return is the first big step in creating cities surrounded by wilderness. Ecological managers, biologists, ecologists, urban planners (or urban de-planners), and others would be needed to help transform the region into an ecological wonder. Buffalo will not repopulate grasslands without assistance. Fences, roads, power lines, and other man-made structures will have to be removed. This could take time, but it is already beginning to happen, even without help.

The exodus of humans from the prairies is resulting in a similar response from nature as when beavers abandon their ponds. Animals that have been absent for decades (even a century) are just wandering back into the land. Grizzly bears are being spotted, cougars are hunting the open fields, and pronghorn are migrating into the non-human plains. With a little help, the Great Plains would be as biodiverse and exciting as the Serengeti of Africa. From the Serengeti plains in Tanzania to the Maasai Mara in southwestern Kenya, over 1.4 million wildebeests, 200,000 zebra, and hundreds of thousands of gazelle migrate across the African landscape in search of food and water. Tourism in Tanzania alone brings nearly 700,000 tourists annually to see the parade of wildlife.[14] Overall, visitors to Tanzania generate more than $1 billion per year for the country and create thousands of jobs.[15] If the Great Plains were restored, the number of species throughout the prairies could dwarf that in Africa. Millions of bison, pronghorn, and other ungulates once roamed those lands. If they were reintroduced, the greatest migration in the world would be in the United States—probably twice the size of anything in Africa. Their return would pay dividends. The return of wolves to Yellowstone has fostered between $35 million and $70 million of economic stimulus in Montana, Idaho, and Wyoming.[16] The drama seen in Africa of lions, cheetah, and other predators hunting prey would be replicated in America, except the predators would be wolves, grizzlies, and cougars. Literally billions in revenue are waiting for the region. Plus, getting to the Great Plains would be easier for Americans than getting to Africa—faster and safer. A flight into a major airport like Houston, Denver, or Chicago would put you at the edge of the plains, and within hours of seeing an ecological spectacle like no other. Another benefit besides the economic ones would be that the prairies would act as a sink for carbon, storing the greenhouse gas naturally. No devices, tanks, or technology needed to filter it—nor anything that would need to be maintained like our current infrastructure systems. That is not to say no technology whatsoever would be needed, just the opposite. Monitoring systems and sensors could be employed to mirror the real world to the computer interfaces in order to help scientists and the general public see how the restoration efforts are improving their lives. The restoration could be a catalyst for allowing the Ogallala Aquifer to refill, which could prove essential if climate change affects the Great Lakes as predicted.

The exodus from rural areas to urbanized centers is happening not just in America. Another place this is happening is Saxony, Germany. Located on the eastern edge of Germany at the border of Poland, it is suffering serious population losses as its young people move to the more economically vibrant western half of the country. The problems outlined earlier with regard to depopulation can be seen throughout the region. Just like in the Great Plains, animals are finding their way into the depopulated areas. As far back as 1995, wolves have been moving in. One lone wolf crossed over from Poland to establish a territory centered at a military training area in northern Saxony. By 2000, the one wolf had found a mate and had pups. Each year since, the pair has had a litter of pups. A second mating pair established themselves in the territory in 2002. Between Poland and Germany, biologists with the International Union for Conservation of Nature and Natural Resources have counted 50 individuals. That number is just enough to allow them to sustain a healthy population for a short time. More will have to be added to avoid problems like inbreeding down the road. Wolves are keystone species, and their presence is always necessary to establish healthy ecosystems. For now, they will serve a different function for the people in Germany and Europe. Wolves are not the only large carnivores returning to their former habitats. Brown bears, wolverines, and lynx have all begun to recolonize areas they have not been present in for hundreds of years. As the European landscape continues to empty, this trend will increase. Even though the surrounding rural landscape has been greatly emptied by people moving to western Germany, the land is still highly modified and domesticated. The IUCN estimates that there are nine separate populations of wolves with permanent packs—in northwest Iberia in Spain, the Baltics and Karelia in Russia, scattered across the Carpathian Mountain range, and throughout the Italian peninsula.[17] The Saxony wolves are highly isolated and within a heavily fragmented area, making it that much harder for the group to gain a foothold in the area. It is not only their limited habitat that threatens their survival—it is also their limited genetic pool. This can be dangerous in two different ways: wolves too isolated will inbreed and genetic deformities will wipe them out, or they will mate with domesticated dogs, forming a hybrid species. If the genetics of hybridized lupus then enter into the larger population of wolves, then over time European wolves would disappear though their half-domestic and half-wild relatives could be abundant. Some of the Saxony wolves are already showing signs of hybridization.

If Western Europe ever truly wants to be a thriving ecosystem again, officials and citizens will have to start by protecting and encouraging the wolves that have reentered the rural lands of Poland and eastern Germany. The European community has set guidelines to help conserve and increase their numbers. It is illegal to shoot wolves for any reason in Germany, and efforts are currently under way by a multinational coalition to build

Figure 24   Red wolves are native to the East Coast of the United States and act as a keystone species in the forests of places such as North Carolina. Credit: US Fish and Wildlife Service

wildlife corridors to connect the Saxony wolves with the other packs. This could be seen as the first real-time experiment of humans moving from anti-keystone species to keystone species within a highly developed space.

John Linnell of the Norwegian Institute for Nature Research, who has been involved with the study of the new populations throughout Europe, has been very direct about the conditions Europeans must confront to live more harmoniously with nature. He has written that there is no wilderness left on the greater European continent, only semi-natural habitats fragmented and divided from each other. With no large areas available to restore, such as those in the Great Plains, carnivores can't roam without coming into contact with humans. The challenge is clear: if a balance in nature is truly important to the future of green buildings and a society

dedicated to sustainability, we are going to have to conserve large carnivores in the same landscapes where we live, work, and play.[18]

Wolves have had a bad reputation for centuries. As children, many
learn the story of Little Red Riding Hood before they know their alphabet
or how to count to ten. Fear of wolves is almost universal, and that fear
has caused an outcry from people in eastern Germany. A campaign has
been launched by a group called *Sicherheit und Artenschutz*, or Security
and Species Protection, that the lupus should be shot because they pose a
danger to people and that it is only a matter of time before someone gets
hurt.[19] Hunters such as Joachim Bachmann, who lives in Saxony, do not
see any good coming from wolves in nature. He believes the new packs
will empty the forests of wild sheep and deer, something he and other
hunters feel is their job.[20] Shepherds in the area are fearful that wolves
will kill their animals; however, they are compensated if a wolf kills their
livestock. Increased numbers of the natural predator could have a negative
effect on the hunters that sell deer meat. If wolves reduce the number of
deer, the government could reduce the number of deer someone can collect during a hunt.

In the United States, similar fears and concerns exist. The grey wolf's
return to Yellowstone met with outcries from the public; ranchers feared
that cattle would be slaughtered and fortunes would be lost. Livestock do
get attacked, and people throughout history have been injured and killed
by predatory species—everything from great white sharks to African lions
to grey wolves have sunk their teeth into human flesh. However, in one
year, more people die in car accidents than the number of deaths from
wolves throughout all of history. More than 30,000 people are killed in
automobile accidents in the United States annually.[21] Worldwide, an estimated 1.2 million people are killed in road crashes each year, and as many
as 50 million are injured.[22] Historic records show that wolves, tigers, lions,
bears, and sharks have never gotten close to that number of attacks on
people.[23] There is not much middle ground within the debate over wolves.
In August 2009, I wrote about the Obama Administration delisting grey
wolves as an endangered species. The comments on the post showed that

a clear line has been drawn between "for" and "against" reintroduction efforts. In the United States, ranchers can't shoot wolves unless they catch them in the act of killing a cow or other animal. People like Martin Davis, a fourth-generation rancher in Montana, argue that it is an issue of private property.[24] He asks why they should have to allow a predator onto their land. For him, wolves mean dead livestock, and that means money out of his pocket. He also points out that the two do not mix over the long term. At some point, cattle will be slaughtered. In 2005, wolf predation on livestock was surveyed against other causes of loss. Wolves ranked second to last for deaths. Domestic dogs killed almost five times as many cattle, and vultures killed almost twice as many cattle as wolves did that year. Respiratory problems were the leading cause of fatality to cattle, killing nearly 1.2 million in 2005. The debate on who is right or wrong will not fade away anytime soon. The loss due to sicknesses does point to something more fundamental. Cattle are not evolutionarily equipped to deal with the weather of Montana or the Great Plains, so millions of individuals die as a result. Some ranchers such as Duane Lammer and Ted Turner are finding better species for the harsh climate of the prairies, as I will discuss in Chapter 11. Some form of agreement will have to come about if humans plan to reverse the damage caused to the planet. Old styles of architecture and infrastructure will only get us more of the same things they have given us; maybe it is time to look at a different strategy for ranching too.

The natural world's ability to heal itself does not always highlight why conservation biology must become the central theme of green building in the century to come. Without new techniques within green building that address preserving natural habitats directly, all the energy efficiency or renewable energy will not save them. Buildings, along with roads and farms, still take up the biggest chunk of land in Europe, far more than natural habitat. And for all of the Passive Houses throughout the continent, these structures are doing nothing to help reconnect the fragments of wilderness. We face similar problems here in the United States, and this is why I stress the need to see buildings as more than individual structures. If you green one house in a subdivision of 500 houses, the overall effect is small. The same is true for cities. If you green an entire city, but the surrounding towns and suburbs are not greened, little comes from the effort. The change has to be across the board. As people leave the Great Plains, species are returning. Some restoration of habitats is occurring too. Currently only about 1 percent of the original grasslands are present throughout the region. The prairies can't heal themselves. For a great migration to come back, it will take designers, city planners, landowners, federal and state governments, ecological planners, policy makers, ranchers, and others to chart a course to make it happen. It is the ultimate challenge of greening America. If, in the coming century, we do not get rid of the old idea of seeing ourselves as separate from nature, it will disappear. The prediction of biologists is that 50 to 75 percent of all species will disappear in the next 100 years if something is not done.[25] Moreover, the financial risks from the loss of species and ecosystems are a greater concern for businesses than international terrorism, according to a United Nations report.[26] From soil erosion caused by agricultural chemicals to water shortages and mining pollution, this report, commissioned by the UN Environment Program and its partners, said the decline in biodiversity would have a $10 billion to $50 billion impact on business.[27] To reverse the trend, keystone species have to be within the landscape to regulate populations of other species. Large carnivores, like wolves, are an essential part of nature. If we hope to enjoy the ecological services of such things as clean air and water throughout the twenty-first and twenty-second centuries, we will need to figure out how to give wilderness more space.

Europe is working to address that challenge. The continent has been virtually nature-free for centuries; however, leaders are now trying to integrate all types of species—both big and small—into the fabric of society.[28] It seems fitting that Europe could be the birthplace for a much more radical view of co-habitation, because Western society is often blamed for the wasteful behavior of people around the world. And wolves are not the only species that need to be returned to the landscape for vast wilderness restoration such as the Great Plains. Prairie dogs and songbirds are important too. It is a bold idea to give nature the space to be natural and wild, but nature does not have much of a say in the matter. We have to be the species to change to make it happen. If we decide to let green buildings simply be houses and offices—or use renewable energy and efficient water systems—we are missing the point. The ultimate test of our resolve for a greener, more sustainable world is seeing how nature can make our lives easier, how it can provide water cheaper than technological devices, and how we can serve it so it can service us.

CHAPTER 11

THE GREATEST VISION

We are unsustainable, but so are beavers. As explained in the preceding chapters, these creatures are showing us that unsustainability is not a death sentence as long as we are deeply integrated into the patterns of life in nature. As I have highlighted, some very positive signs show that people get it. They see that nature can be entwined with society. People benefit from more nature, not less. If the Great Plains were restored to their original condition, it would be the largest ecological restoration of its kind in US history, and it would provide enormous ecological benefits for the entire region, and even the planet. The prairies would once again become a healthy watershed, replenishing the Ogallala Aquifer, a much needed source of water in the decades to come. The preservation and expansion of the short grasslands would create the largest national and natural carbon sink, providing free climate security for as long as the lands were undisturbed. These efforts are not merely about the conservation of our natural world. They are the future of the sustainability movement and green building. Restoring the Great Plains, along with restoring the pine forests of the Southeast and preserving the deserts of the Southwest, would go a long way to establish a true plan for water security, protect the value of property, clean the air of dangerous particulates, curb global warming, and generate feasible long-term solutions for the biggest troubles of today and into the next century. Estuaries should take up space up and down both the East and West Coasts. Oysters should be restored everywhere, and regulations of water quality should be based on their ability to provide ecological services. When structures are built according to the natural climates of an area, they use less energy, and so thereby less energy needs to be created. Using daylight instead of artificial light saves electricity. As conventional cities are built up with concrete and buildings, they become hotter in the summertime than the surrounding area. This is called a heat island effect. Hotter conditions make people use more energy for cooling. If natural lands are worked into urbanized cities, tree coverage can reduce heat island effect, thereby eliminating some of the additional energy needed to cool spaces.

Few see the connection between buildings and their footprint on the planet. In the past, we have tried to engineer our way into better living with dams, infrastructure, fossil fuels, and manufacturing. We never grasped just how much we were dependent on the functioning of the planet until it started to break down. Now we have to pay for what we have used, and learn to live with much less, including space. The quiet truth of the depopulation of Middle America is that it is a sign progress is occurring. The reason megalopolises are discussed in this book is not to figure out if they are good or bad but whether we can use them to the benefit of people and the earth or not. There are already 14 mega-regions in the United States. A century from now, there may be more, or there may be less.

What would it take to restore the grasslands to a viable ecosystem? In some parts of the Great Plains, individuals and states are already trying to make it happen. The possibility of full recovery is huge, but those who undertake it would not be the first to tackle a big project that would contribute positively to cities and nature. The depopulation of the Great Plains is just one opportunity for the latest tools in sustainability and green building to combine with conservation biology.

It is unrealistic to imagine a world untouched by human development. Just like the beaver, it is in our nature to cut down trees, divert water, dig canals, build lodging, and have families. But as the Everglades and the Great Plains show, there is a wrong way and a right way to benefit from nature, and great care must be taken when manipulating ecosystems for specific uses. The Great Plains have undergone a much more extensive alteration of their natural landscape than has the Florida example—as noted, only 1 percent of the original grasslands are intact. Plans to inundate the plains with hundreds of wind turbines could spell the next major environmental disaster, causing water shortages, ecological decay, and a huge missed opportunity. Though, as noted, grasslands have a high potential to act as carbon sinks, the disturbance of soils by wind turbine development would only make natural carbon storage harder.[1] Another potential for natural carbon storage is in forests. Researchers have found that forests between 15 and 800 years old can capture much more carbon than they produce.[2] As discussed in Chapter 7, if we use old-growth forests as a way to protect water sources, they could provide a repository for carbon dioxide. However, when forests are disrupted by logging or soil removal, the carbon is released back into the atmosphere.

Architects, urban designers, and planners will need to stop thinking solely of human-made objects and start allowing large tracks of land to age and continue to grow to ensure the superior water delivery system of the earth's watersheds, as well as carbon capture. They will need to transform their focus from creating big, inflexible infrastructure into creating more flexible methods of delivery. The loss of forests sets off problems like erosion, frequent flooding, and clogging of canals, harbors, and the like. As I've explained, the environmental problems of today are very much the results of yesterday's development decisions—buildings, roads, dams, and power sources. Without the reestablishment of such areas, long-term solutions will be difficult, if not impossible, to find.

But wherever such richness of biodiversity and ecology exists, you have the components for integrating ecomimicry as a basis of design. This does not mean artificially simulating ecosystems but rather rebuilding, restoring, and enhancing them to service all species. The reactionary tone of the current green building movement has clouded our vision for a bolder potential of a green future. What would it look like? Imagine a megalopolis snaking across the landscape—it is densely developed, but wildlife corridors cut through it, crisscrossing the mass to connect and reconnect natural areas at the edges and interiors. More people would live in the United States in the future than now, but less land would be occupied. If you were flying over the land at night, the long asymmetrical shape outlining the mega-region would shine through the dark. The lights would be a little less bright though. If it was April or May, and you were flying from Denver to Chicago, you may be able to look out the window and see tens of millions of bison, pronghorn, and other ungulates moving north for greener pastures blanketing the land as far as the eye could see.

The architecture would be designed, not as the sole expression of a designer's soul, but in tune with its surroundings. Roofs would dip to meet the ground; walls would tilt to let daylight in. Once you land, the air would be crisp and clean. Transportation and energy would be based on hydrogen power. The mission for the next 100 years is to make megalopolises as ecologically sound as possible, and to use them as jumping-off points to restore all of the ecological services we require to make our future better. The megacity of today with its concrete sidewalks and skyscrapers may look somewhat the same, but instead of endless cities with endless highways and asphalt, there would be wildlife corridors cutting through the hardness, injecting greenery throughout our lives and connecting like species. We must envision a civilization that wants to bring urban centers and ecosystems into one space, as one place. I have talked about how ecological services can help us. For us to be keystone species, we have to figure out how to serve nature too.

A report by the WILD Foundation released in June 2010 states that new data about the biological world requires a new global perspective for conservation.[3] Assessments by scientists around the world have come to see that to maintain the full range of life-supporting, ecological, and evolutionary processes provided by wilderness such as water quality, air, waste reconstitution, and food stocks requires that a minimum of half of a given eco-region must be protected. This is good news for the residents of Florida because the efforts in the Everglades can restore 50 percent of its original functionality. This is a strong basis to reestablish the goals of architecture—to change the profession from a building-oriented discipline to an ecological perspective. The same is true for sustainability, engineering, construction, and real estate development. All technologies should be graded not by their lack of carbon emissions but by their ability to move us toward saving, reestablishing, and revitalizing at least 50 percent of ecological areas.

The next time you decide to switch one type of lightbulb for another, ask yourself if doing so will help meet the goal of saving at least 50 percent of nature. As I've noted, if sustainability continues to be primarily about new energy technologies solely for the service of people, including clean energy and utility scale renewable installations, all the good intentions of the movement may give us the same outcome as coal and petroleum.

The Natura 2000 Network is one such organization with the focus of preserving 50 percent of nature. Natura brings together all EU Member States with the goal of maximizing the integration of biodiversity through a network of ecologically valuable sites that show high potential to foster unique species as well as a wide variety of life. This includes areas from the Canaries to Crete and from Sicily to Finnish Lapland. Unfortunately, the Natura 2000 Network currently contains only 26,000 sites, representing about 18 percent of the EU territory. Without giving wildlife the freedom to disperse, move, migrate, and exchange genetics and populations within the other 82 percent of the continent, its long-term survival is in serious question. As the program matures, wildlife corridors will be constructed— and as other areas of Europe thin out, bolder steps to restore the ancient forests of Western Europe could be taken. Most people are aware of the extraordinary annual great migration of wildebeest, zebra, and gazelle across the Serengeti-Mara ecosystem in Africa. Similar migrations were part of the precivilized history of France, Germany, and other European countries. Green buildings' role in the coming century is to capture the power of reinstating such actions. A hundred years from now, perhaps European bison numbering in the thousands will traverse the continent on an annual basis as people go about their lives in Paris, Berlin, Rome, and other major cities.

THE BUFFALO COMMONS

The vision of a buffalo commons in the Great Plains is already under way. Some of the ranchers in the Great Plains have taken to owning buffalo instead of cows. As Duane Lammer, manager of the 25,000 acre Triple 7 Ranch near Rapid City, South Dakota, explained for a *USA Today* interviewer, buffalo are part of the landscape and have been for a very long time.[4] The ranch owners have spent time to understand how to work with the land versus trying to muscle it into doing what they think it should do—and the buffalo do just that. For one, the bison have evolved to deal with the temperatures, harsh conditions, and windy climate of the plains. Fewer of them die from winter weather as well as respiratory issues. The fur and skin of the buffalo keep it comfortable in freezing weather, and they huddle together for extra body heat. The Triple 7 Ranch has more than 1,500 head of buffalo—and other ranchers are starting to see the potential for profit with the other red meat. Ted Turner has nearly 2 million acres of land in seven states (Colorado, Kansas, Montana, Nebraska, New Mexico, South Dakota, and Oklahoma). He is already raising buffalo to stock his chain of restaurants—Ted's Montana Grill—with a beef alternative. He has also begun offering big-game hunting on his ranches like the Flying D, more than 100,000 acres in size, where you can bring down a bison if you desire. Giving people the chance to interact with native beasts like buffalo could help people see a vision of a great migration of them in America. It seems that they are stuck in the historical Wild West. Hunters and environmentalists need to see eye-to-eye to make real change happen, and giving them a firsthand experience with bison could help vitalize a new future story of the Wild West. The Poppers, whom we met in the preceding chapter, in their 1987 essay entitled "The Great Plains: From Dust to Dust," called for the Great Plains to be without fences or boundaries to allow the landscape to return to its natural state.[5] The spirit of a buffalo commons is to take the time necessary to reestablish and reconnect prairie wildland and ecological corridors for all of the native and endemic species—such as bison and grizzly bear—and to do it in a way sustainable for both people and the land for the long term. Conservationists, biologists, and ecologists consider the Great Plains to be as valuable an eco-region as the Galápagos Islands, Congo Basin, and the islands of Borneo and Sumatra—all of which are listed as high-priority areas for conservation.

In a world quickly modernizing and pushing nature out of our daily lives, it can be hard to truly connect with the importance it has. Often, people find it difficult to understand how conservation measures are connected to architecture. That is because buildings have, for most of history, been the tool of fighting nature. For example, when someone clears a large acreage of woodland to build a subdivision, it has been seen as progress. New homes for sale and newly paved roads replace trees and ecology. We rarely look at cities such as Milan, Tokyo, or New York City and realize that what was once there were forests, biodiversity, and nature. We usually only think about the pace of life in an urban area or the expense of living in such a locale. Low-flow toilets and CFL lightbulbs, electric cars, and other technology have only promised to reduce the impact on the environment—and in that, they do a decent job. The preservation of biodiversity is the acid test for how successful we are. We cannot have biodiversity without vast wilderness—that is why we will need to adapt to the changing of the growth of megalopolises, the shrinking of cities, and the need for ecological restoration and technological advancement. As noted, real estate developers will always call on designers to do jobs cheaply and quickly—it is in their nature, just as flooding forests is in the nature of the beaver. It is not technology or ecology—it must be both, but the important point is that ecology must always come first. Taking the journey from where green building is today to where it can be in a century is our great migration—and it could mean our overcoming our role as the anti-keystone species.

CHAPTER 12

OUR ROLE AS A KEYSTONE SPECIES

Big challenges are met by individuals as well as individual actions. Where we will be in a century depends on what we do every day until then. A decade into the twenty-second century will be an interesting time, regardless of whether we accept our place in the natural world or not. Accepting it will help us tweak our influence within the world. Not doing so could be very destructive to us and the earth. I will refrain from further doomsayer talk, especially at this point in the book, but discovering the devastating effect we are having on living organisms is easy to find—you need only consult Google for a bit of research on the subject.

You may be wondering if there are any general rules, guidelines, or practices that you can follow to help bring about the change necessary. I believe there are many. The topics discussed in this book, like the energy grid, megalopolises, and climate change, are big. It can seem as if we are all powerless over the decisions of how a highway is built or how a city is planned or how we need to rethink putting thousands of wind turbines in the middle of America. The coming age of the megalopolis is especially daunting.

Fortunately, green buildings have come a long way since the Earth Summit in Rio in 1992. Having the option to buy nontoxic carpeting, paints, and furniture is a big improvement from not having the option at all. Every house, office, restaurant, church, mosque, school, store, and apartment building should do at least that much. Every building should strive to be as energy and water efficient as possible. Common toxic compounds used within building materials should be outlawed, especially when there is a nontoxic option available.

Currently around 4,000 green buildings exist, with 30,000 more projected to be built in the next ten years. This is, frankly, weak: it needs to be more like 3 million in ten years. Thankfully, more people know that they can pick better buildings to live, work, and play in. Green building is one of the hottest topics in society today, so awareness is still evolving. In the past, architecture was about form and function—today it has become about sustainability and efficiency. There are many resources for people to learn more about the green building of today like the Passive House Institute, International Living Building Institute, Green Globes, the US Green Building Council, Built Green, and many other organizations around the country and the world. It is fairly easy to find conferences, events, and classes to help you know how to make your project as state of the art as possible.

If you are planning to build a new home or office, remember, architecture is client based, so that means architects, engineers, contractors, construction managers, and designers work for you, not the other way around. So going green is really your responsibility. If you have a project and your team tells you that doing a green building is going to be more complicated or cost more money, fire your team. Green building should never be more expensive. I have worked on both big and small projects that had incredibly thin budgets, and the team was more than able to give the client a green building far beyond their expectations. If the team you have is not experienced enough with green design to creatively solve problems, change teams. Many of the groups mentioned above have directories of professionals in your area who can help you through the process of going green. Educate yourself, and ask lots of questions before you hire someone. It really is the difference between being healthy or sick, for both you and the environment.

Of course it will take more than just building green buildings faster than ever before. A new approach to energy will have to be envisioned if we hope to reduce the damage to the earth through burning coal and gasoline. Unfortunately, some so-called green leaders see nuclear energy as a viable and safe choice, despite the damage it causes the environment in the life-cycle analysis. Others think that carpeting the landscape and disrupting fragile ecosystems with solar panels and wind turbines will solve the problems of energy usage. But the problem is not energy alone. The problem is that buildings waste too much energy—too much during operation, too much in the making of their materials, and especially too much in bringing the energy from the utility company to the buildings themselves. Renewable energy is growing fast, but not fast enough in the United States. The slow rate at which we are installing new types of energy, as well as the call for plug-in electric cars, will guarantee that coal and nuclear plants will be around for a long time.

In the long run, advocacy for utility scale projects, renewable or nuclear, will only make it harder to convert to on-site energy generation options like solar and hydrogen. On-site energy generation can be expensive, but it doesn't have to be. The best way to combat that is by designing buildings that need far less energy to begin with. The potential to save between 60 and 80 percent of energy for houses is an essential part of solving the problems that come from fossil fuels and infrastructure. The technology can't be relegated to just residential buildings. It will need to be adapted to commercial and other building types too.

Fuel cells will be on the market for homes within the next two to five years; they are already being used in a handful of homes. So the planets do seem to be aligning for three pivotal things to happen in the coming years. First, green building will bring down the amount of energy needed in a building. Second, smaller and more affordable fuel cells will be produced; and third, the general public will not want to spend hundreds of billions of dollars on an expensive and unreliable smart grid.

But do not stop there—if you do, it is only halfway. Bigger issues are afoot that need serious attention if we intend to still have nature, wilderness, and biodiversity in 100 years. Find out everything you can about groups like the Property & Environmental Research Center,

EcoTrust, Society for Conservation Biology, Rewilding Institute, The Nature Conservancy, Defenders of Wildlife, and the National Geographic Society. These groups take on issues that the green buildings of today are not yet addressing like fragmentation, species extinction, habitat restoration, and watershed protection, and they are proposing interesting answers.

Along with national organizations, there are local alliances, institutes, and affiliates that deal with much more specific topics that are related to the conservation, preservation, and restoration of ecosystems throughout the country. If you investigate all your options, and still do not find what you are looking for, start an organization yourself to deal with filling the gap between nature and buildings, or wilderness and urbanization. Funding is available for such start-ups. The EPA program called Community Action for a Renewed Environment is a competitive grant program that offers an innovative way for a community to organize and take action to reduce toxic pollution in its local environment. The National Oceanic and Atmosphere Administration, The Nature Conservancy, and others also offer financial assistance in creating community-oriented groups to confront ecological preservation and renewal. The green building movement needs passionate, smart, motivated people to bring leading-edge solutions that combine green buildings and conservation.

But most importantly, how do we live more harmoniously within nature, as part of *nature?* The entire history of our civilization has been a story pitting us against nature. All cities, buildings, towns, neighborhoods, and highways are testament to how we view ourselves as separate from the natural world. We are nature, as natural as beavers and oysters. But we have to deal with our bad habit of simplifying ecosystems when we are present and the tendency to destroy more than we heal. So, it is not enough to ask how we can build green or go green. We must ask how we can rebuild and revitalize nature—that is the true question needing attention if we ever hope to make our civilization truly sustainable.

Ecomimicry could be adapted, implemented, and thus overtake the status quo within a decade. As noted, with less than a decade of work with

Forever Florida, big steps forward have been taken in the restoration of the Everglades. Species have reappeared and water quality has improved for people. The wetlands are revitalized, creating natural storm protection and flood control. The architecture and construction worlds need to see that these types of projects are the key to how megalopolises could adapt to meet the challenges of tomorrow.

What we do tomorrow and how green building matures in the next 100 years will inform what comes next. The Great Plains could be alive with millions of bison within a ten-year time, along with wolves, bear, pronghorn, prairie dogs, and others species. Green building could provide a new solution for the region's water by eliminating wasteful industries and replacing them with more ecologically sensitive proposals. By working with landowners and developing an action plan for implementation, designers could see this vision become as real as anything today.

The Great Plains is not the only area in need of restoration. Every region and every country needs serious reform because of how urbanization and human development interfere with nature and ecosystems. Sadly, even if we move with lightning speed, some species will still go extinct—that is the bad news. The good news is that we, as individuals, are not completely powerless and have plenty of things we can do to start saving the biodiversity of our planet, one at a time.

You can start in your backyard. It is not just buildings that are taking up space. Meadows and wooded areas are interrupted by plots of land not only covered by a house but also flanked by a front and backyard carpeted in green grass. It is the same story in just about every neighborhood in the United States. If you use Google Earth to scan the planet, you will be shocked to see just how many yards there are surrounding a house like a SWAT team at a bank robbery. Lawns, as it turns out, are dramatically anti-keystone: you can take a lush habitat full of a wide variety of species that are connected within a complex network of ecological systems and within days transform it into a monoculture of one species of grass.

Professor Ilkka Hanski, of the University of Helsinki in Finland, has done as much as one person can do to help us understand how the fragmentation of natural landscapes due to human development affects populations of species. When he recognized just how much space lawns take up, he hatched a radical plan to see what could be done, and he started in his own backyard, a small plot at less than half an acre. His idea was simple—what would happen if for one year he stopped cutting his grass or engaging in any gardening or cultivation, and let nature take its course.

At the beginning of the experiment, he surveyed his landscape to determine mathematically how many different plants and animals were present. After several hours of combing the topography, he added his findings and concluded that only two species were present. From that point for the next 12 months, he did very little to his yard except watch it grow out of control. He quite enjoyed the ease of having a yard that needed no maintenance, though his neighbors did not seem to like him making his lawn a laboratory. He sent me a photograph of it. In the background, Hanski is standing in the threshold of his backdoor peering at the camera—and in the foreground instead of the typical yard of inch-high grass is an assortment of plants, bushes, and shrubs crowding the area.

After the year was over, he had a third party evaluate what had transpired. From the photograph, it was easy to see that more than two species were now growing on his plot of land. But when the independent analysis was submitted for review, even Hanski was surprised. More than 373 plants and animals were now present on his little piece of earth—two of which were red-listed as potentially endangered. Quite a testimonial for what one can do for nature by simply letting one's yard run wild.

This shows how everyone can participate in restoring species. The practice of ecological landscaping is already part of the efforts of isolated green building projects. Incentive programs, like those already used to encourage energy and water efficiency, could be developed to encourage even more ecological sustainability. Previously, I discussed the idea of using green roofs as a method to connect fragmented lands—but creating wildlife corridors, by way of communities allowing part or all of their backyards to go natural, is something that any home owner can get started on today. If done in coordination with water management and watershed protection, and with the input of ecologists, entire towns could retool their idea of what a yard "should" look like to create easements through-out neighborhoods for natural hydrological water flow and wildlife move-ment. The benefits would include better water security, less expense to the owners for maintenance, and more biodiversity and carbon seques-tration. Property tax reductions and other incentives could be based on how well communities connect their revitalized yards with each other as well as how long they allow their areas to grow free. In the future, entire communities, suburbs, and regions would collaborate to form a mammoth network of backyards interconnecting with other communi-ties, suburbs, and regions to form continental-scale wildlife corridors, watersheds, and easements.

I personally do not believe that government needs to do all the work for people to create a better, more sustainable and ecological world. However, I do think it should do its part. Find out who your representatives are, and contact their offices—whether governor, mayor, senator, or council mem-ber. Find out how they truly feel and believe about issues surrounding the environment. See if they are for or against nuclear power, if they are for or against biodiversity, and if they are for or against ecological sustainability, cleantech, green buildings, and other topics. If they are against them, try to help them better understand the issues. If they still do not feel these subjects are important or do not create laws, legislation, or regulatory direction to help improve the situation—remember politics is voter based. You can work to get them out of office as easily as you can work to help them stay in it. The same is true for companies, corporations, and busi-nesses. Approach them, try to work with them to better their products, their services, their manufacturing processes—whatever it is that they do, help them do it better. If they are unwilling to change, speak with your wallet and stop purchasing their products, find more ecologically friendly products, and buy those instead. Every conceivable item or product from building materials to baby toys has a green alternative today. Embrace cooking things from scratch when there is not a healthy option, use a reusable bottle, buy green energy, and live as green as possible—that kind of stuff is much easier than it once was (but remember that it is only half-way). When looking for a green product that is needed but can't be found locally, go online to search for it, and when you find it, order it and have it shipped to you. Vote with your wallet, speak with your purchases, and lead by example. Such actions can change minds, make companies change processes, and effect change quickly.

But you can't purchase your way into better highways, energy grids, or water delivery. Infrastructure is much bigger than that, and will be much harder to fix. Change will have to be in the form of public and private partnerships. Get involved! We have a deficit of neighborhood groups working toward ecological ends. Community involvement is essential. Work to make highway projects more transparent. Find a local watershed protection group to help your community to rethink how storm water and waterworks are developed and built. The Center of Watershed Protection and the Low Impact Development Center can help you learn about how you can get involved with your community regarding water protection. During my involvement with green buildings and habitat restoration, I met many passionate people incredibly active in both green design and ecology—single moms, teachers, Boy Scout troops, artists, home owners, designers, and many others who juggle responsibilities like family, work, owning small businesses, working full-time, and going to school while still finding the time to be involved with their communities.

Be the inspiration that you want to find, and by any means necessary, educate yourself about ecology, ecomimicry, and conservation biology. There are so many topics that I could not cover in this book that I would love to talk about—things like biogeography, genetic ecology, rewilding, and many others. The more you learn, the better you will understand how and why society needs to focus first on ecology and second on technology. We are all responsible for the future of our planet.

This is not a call for the end of technology but rather for it to be put in the service of the natural world, rather than forcing nature into subservience. Ecosystem solutions will enhance the positives of green buildings by making them more dependent on their surrounding climate as well as more effective in saving energy and water as well as providing comfortable interiors and usability by occupants. The more cities can integrate and restore the surrounding ecology, the better the air and water quality will be. The more building materials can be created with natural processes, the less pollution will be the aftermath of their creation.

If I had to boil it down to three essential points, they would be: water first, habitat second, growth third. Water first because if we manage water correctly, it will guide us to consider habitat, human health, and other species from the beginning. Habitat is a key part to healthy ecosystems. Healthy ecosystems are a key part to ecological services. Habitats are also what we are all a part of, and maintaining them will be a big step forward. By growth, I mean economic growth. The financial reality of modern society is that we are all connected by money, too. It is very important and has to be one of the top three decision factors. That means that everything we build, including homes, cities, cars, plywood, paints, lightbulbs, or interstate highways, should first address its role in the protection of water resources. Second, we need to make sure that growth is geared to restoring habitat. Ask questions like, which species are going to benefit from a bridge, port, statue, or megacity? What is it giving back to nature, and how is the project giving nature the space to be natural and wild? Once those two issues are answered, the third topic can be addressed, which is growth. We are a species obsessed with, and dependent on, growth. It will be very important to make sure we make the decisions that move forward the progress of society.

The green buildings of today must not be the green buildings of tomorrow. In tomorrow's world, we need much greener buildings than we have today—and more of them. In the distant future, we need ecomimicry as the prevailing method for creating things. After that? Greener still. There is no limit to what ecology can teach us, nor what we can do as a society with effective tools to create a sustainable world. Our greatest gift is ourselves, as long as we find the path to being a keystone species.

ACKNOWLEDGMENTS

The convention of literary works is that there is but one author—and along with that comes the notice that he or she sits in front of a keyboard to scribe all the words, sentences, and pages that make up a book. Nothing is farther from the truth. It is a team effort from the very moment an idea is scribbled on a piece of paper until the volume is downloaded to an iPad, smartphone, or Nook (or, of course, bought as a hardcopy in a bookstore or online). I have an extraordinary team of talented and supportive people who are as much the reason for this book existing as I am. First, two very important team members are Palgrave Macmillan and my editor, Luba Ostashevsky. They saw potential in what I thought needed to be said, and gave me the chance to write it for others to read. I am eternally grateful to them. Luba and her assistant Laura Lancaster did for me what I find impossible: they edited my rough drafts into a coherent collection of chapters and parts. From the beginning, I knew their comments and suggestions would ultimately make my work better, and they proved me right. Another very important person on my team is my agent, Kirsten Neuhaus. She has been with this project from nearly the very start—and whipped my original proposal into something a publisher could take seriously. She shepherded me through the gantlet of challenges necessary to truly be published. I cannot say enough great things about her—but the one thing I should say here is that I know that without her talent as an agent my talent as a writer would still be fairly unknown.

The topics of infrastructure, green architecture, conservation biology, and ecological services are subjects that take up libraries on their own. I engaged in a large amount of research to pin down many of the ideas covered. I reviewed and read many books, articles, and blogs. I also did some old-fashioned cold calling and called a long list of people during the process of writing each chapter. I probably called around 100 people—left countless messages explaining why I was calling and what I was hoping to speak with them about. Many people did not return my call. But for those who did, they brought into my work a world of passion and understanding that my experience alone could not match. These people are scattered across the country and planet in fields as diverse as everything from water conservation to urban design to plumbing. I loved talking with all of them—especially the scientists, such as John Beyer, Josh Donlan, Illka Hanski, Viviana Ruiz, Richard Levins, Reed Noss, John M. Marzuluff, and Clive Jones. I am a green designer by profession, but a biologist at heart. Many of these people I have read for years, and I always eagerly searched for new articles and books they may have produced. To have the opportunity to learn what they know one-on-one was a wonderful treat. These people took the time to explain complex topics such as the behavior of pronghorn, metapopulation, evolutionary genetics, and ecological engineers. They pointed my attention to how the biological world is impacted by buildings and roads in ways green building is not addressing. They taught me what no architect or engineer can—that is, the role of nature as nature. I would also like to thank Craig Packer and Hadas Kushnir for explaining the details of lions in Africa as well as Suzanne Stone for taking my two dozen telephone calls asking and re-asking questions regarding wolves in Yellowstone, Michigan, and other parts of the United States. More needs to be written about apex predators, urban space, and infrastructure and how the future of water and energy security is dependent on ecological services being reconstructed and protected. I did my best in my first attempt to show that the future of architecture is much more about ecology than about concrete or steel. The world is in good hands as long as these ecologists are working on the many issues facing our earth.

On the urbanization, design, and architecture side of the book, I was so impressed with all the professionals who gave their time to talk with me about their opinions about green building, water budgeting, urban design, and other topics I covered in the book. Specifically, I would like to thank Wendall Cox, Ken Yeang, Amory Lovins, Martin Melosi, Adam Yarinsky, Dara Zycherman, Ellen Dunham-Jones, Jason McLennan, Kazys Varnelis, Tim Rieniets, and Petra Todorovich. Cox was a fierce advocate for providing data and sources for topics around urbanization, suburbs, growth of cities, and such. Yeang also found that I can be quite annoying when I'm trying to understand something. He took my many calls, referred me to books, and met with me to talk about green building, eco-master planning, and green infrastructure. My approach to green design has been forever influenced for the better—and his words guided many of mine throughout the book. It was also an honor to have a chance to speak directly with Lovins. He was a pioneer when I first got involved with green building—and he is still pioneering new ground.

Mayor Jay Williams spent time speaking with me about Youngstown, Ohio, and the plan to readjust the city. The work he is doing there is inspirational and will become the benchmark for hundreds of other cities and towns facing the changes caused by globalization, megalopolises, and population redistribution over the next few decades. Everyone interested in sustainability needs to study how Youngstown is confronting the infrastructure from the last century in our new century. Also, Vance Martin, the WILD Foundation, Energy Information Agency, Abby Tucker, Dustin Rubenstein, David Baron, Marcus Hall, Frank Popper, Allysia Angus, Robert Bryce, Helen Sarakinos, Aaron Levinthal, Gill Holland, Brian Richter, Mark DeLay, Marco Keiner, Stefan Doering, and Kaid Benfield all contributed their time and ideas to me during my research for the book. These people are experts in fields ranging from biofuel generators to dam removal to green architecture and energy policy. Baron explained the dynamic of people living too close to nature and how, when we live too close, we are turning it into something that is less natural. He gave me an in-depth look at the real danger of living with cougars and other big predators. Levinthal was instrumental in providing me with the components to see just how valuable on-site biofuel can be for the future. Popper was gracious enough to provide me with emails of articles and spoke with me on several occasions about the Great Plains, Buffalo Commons, and other topics regarding the restoration of the vast prairies in Middle America. Special thanks to Meaghan O'Neill and Lloyd Alter from treehugger.com. They have given me the space within my posts to encourage me to write what I believe versus writing what is polite. Without that freedom, this book would have been much more timid and far less useful for the future. I'm grateful to them all.

My friends and family were part of my team in ways less professional but just as important. I would like to thank Josh Dorfman and Joel Fitzpatrick for their friendship. Before I finished my original proposal, and before I ever had an agent, Fitzpatrick was encouraging me to keep going. Dorfman has been ceaselessly generous with his experience as an author and a fellow greenie. Never asking for anything in return, he helped me believe I could actually get a book deal and write this book. I would also like to acknowledge David Bois, Lauren Spencer, Nora Simpson, Céleste Lilore, Tim Brandoff, and Jerrold Mundis. These people are also my friends. In big and small ways, they assisted me when they had nothing to gain from it. They opened their Rolodex when I was searching for experts to interview about specific topics. Bois and Spencer stepped up in the darkest hours of my writing and provided editing and copy that created the final manuscript of this book. Bois helped with an entire chapter while I frantically tried to rewrite the others. With little more than a phone call and an email, Bois grasped the context of the chapter and turned it into something great. Both Bois and Spencer gave me the boost (literarily and morally) I needed to wrap this book up by the deadline. Brandoff and Mundis, two fellow writers, offered suggestions in avoiding writer's block and the pitfalls of over-thinking the process. Essentially, they told me to keep writing…just keep on writing. I am very grateful for my friends as they played an important role in this journey.

Lastly, I would like to thank my family. My brother Parker Chambers, my mom and dad, as well as Jack and Beverly Fellin—they have all influenced my undying will to try my best to save the world. The most important member on my team is my beautiful and wonderful wife, Lucy Chambers. She started this journey with me as Lucy Jones. For months, I wrote nearly every day. I had to reschedule vacations and dates with her because of deadlines and timeframes. She gave me the love and under-standing that kept me going when I thought finishing the book was just too much to accomplish. She encouraged me, read first drafts, edited my messy grammar, and helped me see when I was being too technical. She also got me out of my chair and from in front of my computer to enjoy the day or afternoon with walks to Central Park or coffee breaks at our favorite neighborhood cafés. She made sure I ate well when I was too deep into writing that I forgot about breakfast, lunch, and dinner. She makes me a better man, and I know this book is only possible with her in my life.

If I have forgotten anyone, my apologies.

NOTES

CHAPTER 1: WHEN BUILDINGS WENT BAD

1. "Chaco Canyon, New Mexico," Sacred Sites: Places of Peace and Power, Magic Planet Productions, LLC, http://sacredsites.com/americas/united _states/chaco_canyon.html.
2. London Hazards Centre Factsheet, "Asbestos Disease," London Hazards Centre, http://www.lhc.org.uk/members/pubs/factsht/81fact.htm.
3. "An Introduction to Indoor Air Quality (IAQ)," United States Environmental Protection Agency, November 16, 2010, http://www.epa.gov/iaq/voc.html# Health%20Effects.
4. Natural Living, "Is Your Carpet Toxic?" Natural Living: Simple Living, Going Green and Eco Choices, http://living.amuchbetterway.com/toxic-carpet-dangerous-toxins-that-live/.
5. "Iron Ore Pricing Emerges from Stone Age," *Financial Times*, October 26, 2009, http://metalsplace.com/news/articles/30805/iron-ore-pricing-emerges-from-stone-age/.
6. Bill O'Neill, "Mining the Heart of a Continent," October 29, 1994, http://www.kiwihyde.com/?p=68.
7. Whole Building Design Guide, "Construction Waste," National Institute of Building Science, http://www.wbdg.org/references/mou_cw.php.
8. Lorette Hall, "Aluminum," How Products Are Made, Volume 5, 2006, http://www.madehow.com/Volume-5/Aluminum.html.

CHAPTER 2: THE HISTORY OF GREEN BUILDING

1. Charles Kibert, *Sustainable Construction: Green Building Design and Delivery* (Hoboken, NJ: John Wiley & Sons, Inc., 2008), 48.

2. Staff of National Oceanic and Atmospheric Administration Paleoclimatology Program, "North American Drought: A Paleo Perspective," National Oceanic and Atmospheric Administration Paleoclimatology Program, November 12, 2003, http://www.ncdc.noaa.gov/paleo/drought/drght_home.html.

3. Richard Seager, Alexandrina Tzanova, and Jennifer Nakamura, "Drought in the Southeastern United States: Causes, Variability over the Last Millennium, and the Potential for Future Hydroclimate Change," *Journal of Climate* 22 (October 1, 2009).

4. Randy Serraglio, "Study Shows Water Shortages in Southeast United States Are Due to Overpopulation, Likely to Be Repeated," Center for Biological Diversity, October 19, 2009, http://www.biologicaldiversity.org/news/press_releases/2009/water-shortage-10-19-2009.html.

5. Wendy Koch, "Global Warming Raises Water Shortage Risks in One-Third of U.S. Counties," July 20, 2010, http://content.usatoday.com/communities/greenhouse/post/2010/07/global-warming-raises-water-shortage-risks-in-one-third-of-us-counties/1.

6. Solar Expert, "History of Solar Power," AMECO, http://www.solarexpert.com/pvbasics2.html.

7. Rainforest Relief, "Avoiding Unsustainable Rainforest Wood," Rainforest Relief, 2007, http://www.rainforestrelief.org/What_to_Avoid_and_Alternatives/Rainforest_Wood.html.

8. National Water Quality Inventory, US Environmental Protection Agency, Office of Water, Washington, DC, August 2002.

CHAPTER 3: HOW INFRASTRUCTURE MAKES WATER WORK FOR US

1. "Water Science for Schools: Water Q&A: Water Use," United States Geological Survey, last modified December 14, 2010, http://ga.water.usgs.gov/edu/qausage.html.

2. "Making Every Drop Count," *The Economist*, November 4, 2010, 62:8.

3. Abby Rockefeller, "Sewage Treatment Plants vs. the Environment," http://www.ejnet.org/sludge/treatment.html.

4. "Combined Sewer Overflows Demographics," United States Environmental Protection Agency, http://cfpub.epa.gov/npdes/cso/demo.cfm.

5. "Water Science for Schools: Water Withdrawals in the U.S. in 2000," United States Geological Survey, http://ga.water.usgs.gov/edu/totpie95.html.

6. "River Facts," American Rivers, http://www.americanrivers.org/library/river-facts/river-facts.html.

7. "Great Lakes Facts and Figures," Great Lakes Information Network, http://www.great-lakes.net/lakes/ref/lakefact.html.

8. C. Michael Hogan, PhD, "Water Pollution," The Encyclopedia of Earth, http://www.eoearth.org/article/Water_pollution?topic=58075.

9. "Columbia River History: Extinction," Northwest Power and Conservation Council, June 2010, http://www.nwcouncil.org/history/Extinction.asp.

10. National Water Quality Inventory, US Environmental Protection Agency, Office of Water, Washington, DC, August 2002.

11. Felicity Barringer, "Lake Mead Could Be within a Few Years of Going Dry, Study Finds," *New York Times*, February 13, 2008, http://www.nytimes.com/2008/02/13/us/13mead.html.

12. "Scientific Facts on Arsenic," Green Facts, http://www.greenfacts.org/en/arsenic/l-2/arsenic-7.htm.

13. "Health Security through Healthy Environments: Facts and Figures Focus on Africa," First Inter-Ministerial Conference on Health and Conference in Africa, http://www.unep.org/health-env/pdfs/Media_FactFigures.pdf.

14. Duncan Graham-Rowe, "Hydroelectric Power's Dirty Secret Revealed," *New Scientist*, February 24, 2005, http://www.newscientist.com/article/dn7046.

15. "Water Science for Schools: Public-Supply Water Use," United States Geological Survey, http://ga.water.usgs.gov/edu/wups.html.

16. "Water Science for Schools: Thermoelectric-Power Water Use," United States Geological Survey, http://ga.water.usgs.gov/edu/wupt.html.

CHAPTER 4: THE ELECTRICAL GRID

1. Conrad Schneider and Jonathan Banks, "The Toll from Coal: An Updated Assessment of Death and Disease from America's Dirtiest Energy Source," Clean Air Task Force, September 2010, 4, http://www.catf.us/resources/publications/files/The_Toll_from_Coal.pdf.

2. Vijay V. Vaitheeswaran, *Power to the People: How the Coming Energy Revolution Will Transform an Industry, Change Our Lives, and Maybe Even Save the Planet* (New York: Farrar, Straus and Giroux, 2003), 24–29.

3. Richard Harris, "New Grid May Be Needed, But So Is Smarter Use," NPR, May 1, 2009, http://www.npr.org/templates/story/story.php?storyId=103713402.

4. "Visualizing the U.S. Electric Grid," NPR.org, May 1, 2009, http://www.npr
.org/templates/story/story.php?storyId=110997398.

5. Danny Bradbury, "Electric Vehicles Will Accelerate after Slow Start," *business-
Green*, November 2, 2010, http://www.businessgreen.com/bg/news/1870021/
electric-vehicles-accelerate-slow-start.

6. "Annual Energy Outlook 2011 with Projections to 2035," US Energy
Information Administration, December 14, 2009, http://www.eia.doe.gov/
oiaf/aeo/electricity.html.

7. Jon Hughes, "The Nuclear Dossier," *The Ecologist*, July/August 2006, 47–48.

8. "U.S. Energy Consumption by Energy Source," US Energy Information
Administration, August 2010, http://www.eia.doe.gov/cneaf/solar
.renewables/page/trends/table1.html.

9. "Renewable Energy Consumption and Electricity Preliminary Statistics
2009," US Energy Information Administration, August 2010, http://www.eia
.doe.gov/cneaf/alternate/page/renew_energy_consump/rea_prereport.html.

10. Allie Gardner, "Solar Could Supply 10% of U.S. Energy Needs by 2025,"
Clean Energy Authority, October 27, 2010, http://www.cleanenergyauthor-
ity.com/solar-energy-news/study-shows-solar-growth-102710/.

11. Peter Behr, "Predicting Wind Power's Growth—an Art That Needs
More Science," *New York Times*, April 28, 2010, http://www.nytimes.com/
cwire/2010/04/28/28climatewire-predicting-wind-powers-growth----an-
art-that-29171.html.

12. Michael Wang, May Wu, and Hong Huo, "Life-Cycle Energy and Greenhouse
Gas Emission Impacts of Different Corn Ethanol Plant Types," Center for
Transportation Research, Argonne National Laboratory, Institute of Physics
Publishing, May 2007.

13. Wayne Laugesen, "Our View: Electric Cars Burn Coal, Mr. President (Vote
in Poll)," *Colorado Spring Gazette*, June 24, 2010, http://www.gazette.com/
articles/electric-100762-cars-wants.html.

CHAPTER 5: THE SUSTAINABILITY OF NATURE

1. Joseph S. Stroud, "Ogallala Aquifer Starting to Run on Empty," *San Antonio
Express-News*, August 16, 2006, http://www.texaswatermatters.org/pdfs/
news_336.pdf.

2. Ted McLaughlin, "Ogallala Aquifer Gets Outside Help," November 25, 2010, http://www.bestoftheblogs.com/Home/33913.

3. Forrest Wilder, "The Late, Great Ogallala Aquifer: A Closer Look at the Decline of the Panhandle's Greatest Resource," *The Texas Observer*, August 31, 2010, http://www.texasobserver.org/forrestforthetrees/the-late-great-ogallala-aquifer.

4. "Beaver Biology," Beaver Solutions, http://www.beaversolutions.com/about_beaver_biology.asp.

5. "Hoover Dam and the Negative Effects on Environment," SlideShares, http://www.slideshare.net/Lengkengs/hoover-dam-and-the-negative-effects-on-environment-4204612.

6. David B. Goings, "Dams—Impact of Dams," JRank, http://science.jrank.org/pages/1942/Dams-Impact-dams.html.

7. "Fun Facts about Hoover Dam," Nevada Commission on Tourism, http://hooverdam.travelnevada.com/funfacts.aspx.

8. Edward O. Wilson, *The Future of Life* (New York: Alfred A. Knopf, 2002), 160–164.

9. Laura Wilkenson, "Red Wolf Makes Comeback in North Carolina," *Technician*, August 25, 2010, http://www.technicianonline.com/features/red-wolf-makes-comeback-in-north-carolina-1.2308922.

10. "Cold Weather, Overpopulation Leads to Deer Die-Off," Buck Manager, March 16, 2010, http://www.buckmanager.com/2009/03/16/cold-wet-weather-causes-deer-die-off/.

11. "2002 a Record Year for Hemorrhagic Disease," North American Whitetail, http://www.northamericanwhitetail.com/deermanagement/dm_aa026003/index.html#cont.

12. "Red Wolf Recovery Project," United States Fish and Wildlife Service, April 7, 2010, http://www.fws.gov/redwolf/.

CHAPTER 6: THE CITIES OF TOMORROW

1. Yoav Hagler, "Defining U.S. Megaregions," *America 2050*, November 2009, 5–8.

2. Jake Vail, "As the Plains Empty, Minds Change," The Land Institute, 2004, http://www.landinstitute.org/vnews/display.v/ART/2004/03/11/4051f2c4bf199.

3. Cheyenne Wells, "The Great Plains Drain," *The Economist*, January 17, 2008, http://www.economist.com/node/10534077?story_id=10534077.

4. John Anderlik, "Rural Depopulation: What Does It Mean for the Future Economic Health of Rural Areas and the Community Banks That Support Them?" *FDIC Banking Review*, July 1, 2004, http://www.allbusiness.com/finance/958965-1.html; Glen Martin, "Where the Buffalo Roam, Again," *San Francisco Chronicle*, April 22, 2001.

CHAPTER 7: WORKING WITH NATURE TO FIND CLEAN WATER

1. Thomas Harter, "Basic Concepts of Groundwater Hydrology," University of California Division of Agriculture and Natural Resources, Publication 8083, http://groundwater.ucdavis.edu/Publications/Harter_FWQFS_8083.pdf.

2. "Thermal Pollution," The Encyclopedia of Earth, last modified December 20, 2010, http://www.eoearth.org/article/Thermal_pollution?topic=49471.

3. City of New York Department of Environmental Protection website, http://www.nyc.gov/html/dep/html/drinking_water/index.shtml.

4. "Living Building Challenge 2.0: A Visionary Path to a Restorative Future," International Living Building Institute, April 2010, http://ilbi.org/lbc/Standard-Documents/LBC2-0.pdf.

5. Carole Moore, "Intervention with Teeth—and Mussels: Oyster Environmentalists," *Harvard Magazine*, January–February 2005, http://harvardmagazine.com/2005/01/oyster-environmentalists.html.

CHAPTER 8: ENERGY BETTER SIZED

1. Justin Gerdes, "The Future of Smart Grid Transmission: Superconducting High-Voltage Power Lines," Gigaom, February 23, 2010, http://gigaom.com/cleantech/the-future-of-smart-grid-transmission-superconducting-high-voltage-power-lines/.

2. Energy Star, "Did You Know? Light Bulbs (CFLs) for Consumers," US Environmental Protection Agency and the US Department of Energy, http://www.energystar.gov/index.cfm?fuseaction=find_a_product.showProductGroup&pgw_code=LB.

3. "Learn about Mercury and Its Effects," Natural Resource Defense Council, http://www.nrdc.org/health/effects/mercury/effects.asp.

4. "Fluorescent Bulbs: A Better Idea?" *Morning Edition*, NPR, February 22, 2007.

5. "CFL Bulbs Have One Hitch: Toxic Mercury," *All Things Considered*, NPR, February 15, 2007.

6. Kevin Bullis, "Solar-Power Breakthrough," *Technology Review*, July 31, 2008, http://www.technologyreview.com/energy/21155/.

7. David L. Chandler, "New Water-Splitting Catalyst Found," MIT press release, May 12, 2010, http://web.mit.edu/press/2010/nocera-paper.html.

CHAPTER 9: BRIDGING THE DIVIDE BETWEEN BUILDINGS AND WILDERNESS

1. Erica Robbins, "So You Want to Know More About... Plants and Animals of the Everglades," Official Site for the Comprehensive Everglades Restoration Plan, http://www.evergladesplan.org/facts_info/sywtkma_animals.aspx; "Freshwater Fishes," Florida Museum of Natural History Ichthyology Department, http://www.flmnh.ufl.edu/fish/southflorida/everglades/marshes/evergladesfish.html.

2. Steve Trombulak, "How to Design an Ecological Reserve System," *WildEarth*, Special Paper Number 1, 1–19, 1996, http://community.middlebury.edu/~trombula/Reserves.html.

3. Telephone conversation with author, October 4, 2010.

4. US Department of Transportation, Federal Highway Administration, "Highway Statistics Summary to 1995," FHWA-PL-97-009 (Washington, DC: July 1997), Table MV-201.

5. American Public Transit Association, *Public Transportation Fact Book* (Washington, DC, 2010), Appendix A: Historical Tables, Table 17, http://www.apta.com/RESOURCES/STATISTICS/Pages/transitstats.aspx.

6. US Department of Transportation, Federal Transit Administration, National Transit Database, "Annual Data Tables" (Washington, DC, Annual Issues), http://www.ntdprogram.gov/ntdprogram/data.htm.

7. US Department of Transportation, Federal Aviation Administration, *FAA Statistical Handbook of Aviation*, Highway Statistics (Washington, DC, Annual Issues), Table VM-1, http://www.fhwa.dot.gov/policy/ohpi/hss/hsspubs.cfm.

8. G. L. Evink, "NCHRP Synthesis 305—Interaction between Roadways and Wildlife Ecology, National Cooperative Highway Research Program,"

Transportation Research Board, National Research Council (Washington, DC, 2002).

9. University of California, Davis, "Designing Wildlife Corridors: Wildlife Need More Complex Travel Plans," *ScienceDaily*, October 21, 2008, http://www.sciencedaily.com/releases/2008/10/081020135221.htm.

10. A. P. Clevenger, J. Wierzchowski, B. Chruszcz, and K. Gunson, "GIS-Generated, Expert-Based Models for Identifying Wildlife Habitat Linkages and Planning Mitigation Passages," *Conservation Biology* 16, no. 2 (2002): 503–514.

11. J. G. Woods, "Effectiveness of Fences and Underpasses on the Trans-Canada Highway and Their Impact on Ungulate Populations Project," Canadian Parks Service, Natural History Division (Calgary, Alberta, Canada, March 1990).

12. F. G. Bank, C. L. Irwin, G. L. Evink, M. E. Gray, S. Hagood, J. R. Kinar, A. Levy, D. Paulson, B. Ruediger, and R. M. Sauvajot, "Wildlife Habitat Connectivity across European Highways," Report No. FHWA-PL-02-011, United States Department of Transportation Federal Highway Administration (Washington, DC, August 1992).

13. Scott Jackson, "Salamander Tunnels," Critter Crossings: Linking Habitats and Reducing Roadkill, US Department of Transportation, Federal Highway Administration, March 21, 2001, http://www.fhwa.dot.gov/environment/wildlifecrossings/salamand.htm.

14. Russell A. Mittermeier, Cristina Goettsch Mittermeier, Patricio Robles Gil, and John Pilgrim, "37 Wilderness Places," *Wilderness: Earth's Last Wild Places* (Chicago: Conservation International, 2003), http://www.press.uchicago.edu/Misc/Chicago/9686397698.html.

CHAPTER 10: THE INVISIBLE CITY

1. "Making Every Drop Count: Utilities Are Getting Wise to Smart Meters and Grids," *Economist*, November 4, 2010, 8.

2. Hillary Brenhouse, "Plans Shrivel for Chinese Eco-City," *New York Times*, June 24, 2010.

3. Adam Schreck, "Shifting Plans for $22 Billion Clean-Energy City in Middle East," Associated Press, October 10, 2010, http://www.msnbc.msn.com/id/39601848/ns/world_news-world_environment/.

4. "Depopulation: The Great Plains Drain," *Economist*, January 17, 2008, http://www.economist.com/node/10534077?story_id=10534077.

5. Tim Rieniets, telephone conservation with author, July 27, 2010.

6. Jason Daley, "Where to Be an Entrepreneur: The Dreamer: Youngstown, Ohio," *Entrepreneur*, August 2009, http://www.entrepreneur.com/article/ 202666-9.

7. Greg Miller, "Youngstown, Ohio: A Photographer's Journal," *Inc.*, http://www.inc.com/ss/youngstown-ohio-photographer-journal.

8. Robert H. Boyle, "Friends of a Living Fossil," *Sports Illustrated*, March 4, 1996, http://sportsillustrated.cnn.com/vault/article/magazine/MAG1007796/index.htm.

9. Jerry Zremski, "Warming Study Sees Problems for Great Lakes," *Buffalo News*, April 17, 2007.

10. Deborah Epstein Popper and Frank J. Popper, "The Great Plains: From Dust to Dust," *Planning*, December 1987, 12–18.

11. Deborah Popper, Frank Popper, and former Kansas governor Mike Hayden speaking on "The Buffalo Commons Revisited," Kansas State University, February 2004.

12. Daniel C. Fitzgerald, "Ghost Towns of Kansas Volume One," http://www.danielcfitzgerald.com/ghosttowns1.html.

13. Deborah Popper, Frank Popper, and former Kansas governor Mike Hayden speaking on "The Buffalo Commons Revisited," Kansas State University, February 2004.

14. "Ecologist Surprised at Abrupt End to Serengeti-Mara Wildebeest Migration," *Conservation News*, October 25, 2010.

15. "Effects of a Proposed Commercial Route through the Serengeti National Park on Tanzania's Tourist Industry," Serengeti Watch, July 27, 2010, http://www.savetheserengeti.org/news/highway-news/economic-impact-statement/.

16. Dr. James C. Halfpenny, "Wolf Restoration Is Worth Millions of Dollars to the Economies of Idaho, Montana, and Wyoming," Wolf Report, April 16, 2006, http://www.forwolves.org/ralph/wolf-economic-impact.htm.

17. Large Carnivore Initiative for Europe 2006, "Canis lupus," International Union for Conservation of Nature Red List of Threatened Species, Version 2010.4., 2010, www.iucnredlist.org.

18. John D. C. Linnell, Norwegian Institute for Nature Research, Tungasletta-2, N-7485 Trondheim, Norway.

19. "The Return of Wolves to Germany: 'Fears are Being Stoked,'" *Der Spiegel*, February 20, 2007, http://www.spiegel.de/international/spiegel/0,1518, 467205,00.html.

20. Jeffrey Fleishman, "Fangs Are Bared in Germany," *Los Angeles Times*, January 22, 2007, http://articles.latimes.com/2007/jan/22/world/fg-wolves22.

21. Fatality Analysis Reporting System Encyclopedia, National Statistics, National Highway Traffic Safety Administration, 2007, http://www-fars.nhtsa.dot.gov/ Main/index.aspx.

22. Ibid.

23. John D. C. Linndell, *The Fear of Wolves: A Review of Wolf Attacks on Humans* (Trondheim: Norsk Institutt for Naturforskning, January 2002), 18–32.

24. Martin Davis, interviewed by David Brancaccio, *Now*, PBS, August 18, 2006.

25. Gary Strieker, "Scientists Agree World Faces Mass Extinction," *CNN. com/SCI-TECH*, August 23, 2002, http://archives.cnn.com/2002/TECH/ science/08/23/green.century.mass.extinction/index.html.

26. Jonathan Watts, "Biodiversity Loss Seen as Greater Financial Risk than Terrorism, Says UN," *Guardian*, October 27, 2010, http://www.guardian. co.uk/environment/2010/oct/27/biodiversity-loss-terrorism.

27. "Demystifying Materiality: Hardwiring Biodiversity and Ecosystem Services into Finance," UNEP Finance Initiative: Innovative Financing for Sustainability, October 2010, http://www.unepfi.org/fileadmin/documents/ CEO_DemystifyingMateriality.pdf.

28. Large Carnivore Initiative for Europe 2006, "Canis lupus," IUCN 2010, IUCN Red List of Threatened Species, Version 2010.4, www.iucnredlist.org.

CHAPTER 11: THE GREATEST VISION

1. Sebastiaan Luyssaert, Detlef Schulze, Annett Börner, Alexander Knohl, Dominik Hessenmöller, Beverly E. Law, Philippe Ciais, and John Grace, "Old-Growth Forests as Global Carbon Sinks", *Nature* 455 (September 11, 2008): 213–215.

2. Sebastiaan Luyssaert et al., "Old-Growth Forests as Global Carbon Sinks," *Nature* 455 (September 11, 2008): 213–215, www.nature.com/nature/ journal/v455/n7210/full/nature07276.html.

3. The WILD Foundation, "WILD9—The 9th World Wilderness Congress," www.wild.org/main/world-wilderness-congress/wild9/.

4. Haya El Nasser, "Life on the Great Plains Is Anything but Plain, Simple," *USA Today*, August, 13, 2007, http://www.usatoday.com/news/nation/2007-08-12-great-plains_N.htm.

5. Deborah Epstein Popper and Frank J. Popper, "The Great Plains: From Dust to Dust," *Planning*, December 1987, 12–18.

INDEX